EGO

vs.

EQ

EGO
VS.
EQ

- - - - -

HOW TOP LEADERS BEAT
8 EGO TRAPS WITH
EMOTIONAL INTELLIGENCE

JEN SHIRKANI

First published by Bibliomotion, Inc.

33 Manchester Road
Brookline, MA 02446
Tel: 617-934-2427
www.bibliomotion.com

Printed in the United States of America

Library of Congress Cataloging-in-Publication Data

Shirkani, Jen.
   Ego vs. EQ : how top leaders beat 8 ego traps with emotional intelligence /
Jen Shirkani.
      pages cm
   ISBN 978-1-937134-76-1 (hardback) — ISBN 978-1-937134-77-8 (ebook) —
ISBN 978-1-937134-78-5 (enhanced ebook)
   1. Executives—Psychology.   2. Emotional intelligence.   3. Management—
Psychological aspects.   4. Leadership—Psychological aspects.   I. Title.
   HD38.2.S495 2013
   658.4'094—dc23
                                                                2013020744

*This book is dedicated to leaders everywhere who have
the courage to look within.*

Contents

Acknowledgments

I could never have accomplished this without the help of so many supporters.

My family: Steve, Caitlin, and Annie DeWaters, my parents: Jeff Shirkani and Nancy Martin, my sisters: Joy Shirkani-Monson and Dr. Kim Shirkhani.

My advisors: Faith Csikesz, Pamela Sumner, and Steve Calandro.

My support team: Suzanne Murray of Style Matters, Erika Heilman and Jill Friedlander of Bibliomotion, Marilyn Ellis and Jane Mata.

My muses: Thank you to all my amazing clients and colleagues whose generous vulnerability allowed me to share your stories with others. I have been privileged to be part of your journey and am so proud of each of you for your commitment and humility in becoming emotionally intelligent leaders. In particular—NL, RM, JS, DB, TH, GG, RK, MS, BM, CS, SS, and MH—thank you.

Introduction

The Eight Ego Traps

Getting the truth from others when you are in a position of power is tough. It's a tale as old as "The Emperor's New Clothes": No one wanted to tell the emperor he was naked, and no one wants to tell the CEO he might be wrong. Whatever the nature of the feedback for the leader, if it's not purely positive, colleagues, employees, and peers may hesitate to offer it. That lack of candor can quickly lead to trouble: today, tomorrow, or in a few months' time.

No matter how open minded or easy to talk to you may be, having a top executive role requires that you use diligent, mindful effort to stay grounded and in touch with how the decisions you make effect the people on the assembly line making widgets for you every day. Losing touch with the impact you have on others is quite common. And it's inherent in the job. No leader is immune, even in a company with only five people.

Gary, for example, was a brilliant but aloof lawyer who rose through the ranks of his $3 billion company to the position of chief legal officer. When Gary served at lower positions in the company, his colleagues were able to tolerate his cold, impersonal nature—he had excellent technical skills so they were willing to overlook his gruff approach. Once at the post of CLO, however, Gary's direct reports—high-ranking lawyers themselves—were far less tolerant of Gary's insensitive manner and weak interpersonal skills. In a matter of months, Gary's direct reports declared virtual mutiny.

Then there was Jim, a likable CEO with an infectious laugh, who had a tendency to change directives to his team on a whim. Ten days before an internal conference, and after months of planning, Jim directed his senior operations team to bring in a new speaker for the event— a Navy Seal he had just heard on the radio and immediately wanted to hire. The team scrambled to secure the speaker, but the event itself fell flat because planning time ran short and the fit between the male, retired military speaker and the mostly female audience was a poor one. Worse yet, the operations team lost their motivation to work as diligently on future events, knowing that Jim might change the plan at a moment's notice. Company morale and the overall success of the meeting suffered.

These are just two of the leaders who will be featured in this book— individuals facing ego versus EQ challenges (more details on those terms later), challenges that could have cost them their jobs or their company's viability, especially over time. It's hard enough to climb to the top post in an organization or to build a business from the ground up; why make it more difficult to stay there by getting in one's own way? That's what Gary and Jim were inadvertently doing, in spite of being solid business-people who brought many strengths to the table.

The Secret Ingredient: Emotional Intelligence

Although your experiences may not be exactly the same as those of Gary or Jim, these stories highlight some important questions every leader should ask. Whether you are an executive at a large company, VP of the division, or the owner of a small to medium enterprise, now that you've made it to the top, how do you stay there and thrive? How do you ensure growth and results over the long term? And how do you avoid the fate of so many other CEOs who have ultimately gotten fired and business owners whose enterprises have failed in the long run?

Anyone at the top of her organization shudders (if even just a little) when news breaks about a crisis that has occurred on another CEO's watch. Think of the BP oil spill off the coast of Florida, which released nearly 200 million gallons of oil between April and July of 2010.[1] Indicting media images of BP's CEO Tony Hayward vacationing at a yacht race in the middle of the crisis weren't far behind.[2] Then, in 2011, it was media mogul Rupert Murdoch who was thrust into the critical limelight for the phone-hacking scandal at his British tabloid, *News of the World*, which led the parents of a murdered girl to think their daughter might still be alive and checking voice-mail messages.[3,4] More recently, we have seen the once impeccable reputation of JP Morgan Chase's CEO Jamie Dimon tarnished, after answering for at least *$6 billion* in trading losses for the company in May of 2012.[5] Sadly, the CEO blunder is so expected these days that it is now memorialized in *Forbes's* annual report of "Worst CEO Screw-Ups."[6]

No CEO or business owner wants to find himself in that kind of crisis situation, where his reputation is at stake and the future of his organization is put into question. But as we all know, bad things happen to good people and to perfectly good organizations every day. As unfair as it may sometimes be, in the end, there's often only one person who is held responsible: the CEO or business owner.

Let's be a little more optimistic, however, and assume that danger doesn't lurk around the corner for your job title or for your company's long-term security. Let's enjoy a moment in which things are, in fact, going swimmingly. In this fine situation, how do you nonetheless help yourself, your team, and the organization climb still higher? Even at the top, we all want to get a little bit better: to innovate again, to generate higher profits, to contribute to the industry in a meaningful way, and so on. It's your turn now, but how do you do it, not just once but continually?

Enter *EQ,* or *emotional intelligence.* Dr. Daniel Goleman made the concept of emotional intelligence big in 1995, with the publication of his *New York Times* best seller, *Emotional Intelligence: Why It Can Matter More Than IQ,* and since then we've been learning more and more about why emotional intelligence—or the capacity for self-awareness, empathy, social skills, motivation, and self-regulation—is so important. In fact, it's not just important, it's essential. Goleman has found through his extensive research at nearly two hundred large, global companies that EQ is the clear differentiator between those leaders who are successful and those who are not. In particular, Goleman found that emotional intelligence was twice as important as technical skills and IQ for "jobs at all levels."[7] The conclusion? IQ and technical skills are important, but they mean much less without EQ to back them up.

So if emotional intelligence is so vital to effective leadership, what does it really mean to possess this ability? Goleman defines emotional intelligence as "The capacity for recognizing our own feelings and those of others, for motivating ourselves, for managing emotions well in ourselves and our relationships."[8] In my own words, EQ is the demonstration of sensibility. It is a set of skills that includes the ability to *recognize* one's own impulses and moods, *read* situations and others accurately, and *respond* most appropriately, depending on the situation or person involved. Someone with high EQ can communicate with others effectively, can manage change well, is a good problem solver, uses humor to build rapport, has empathy for others, and remains optimistic even in the face of difficulty.

Now let's focus on how EQ looks specifically for individuals at the top of the organization. A leader with high EQ is not threatened by challenges from others, is easy to work with and for, and holds firm performance standards while also being seen as fair and trusting. Leaders with EQ also display situational awareness and emotional connectedness, two vital skills for building employee engagement. And employee engagement is what every executive wants. It is demonstrated by employees who go the extra mile, not because they have to but because they want to and because they feel a profound connection to their leader or their company. Research continues to show that organizations with higher employee engagement levels outperform those with less engaged employees.[9]

The term EQ was first coined in the 1980s by Dr. Reuven Bar-On, who wrote, "Emotional–social intelligence is a cross-section of interrelated emotional and social competencies, skills and facilitators that determine how well we understand and express ourselves, understand others and relate with them, and cope with daily demands, challenges and pressures."[10] Bar-On discovered a key correlation between resiliency and "emotional quotient." Today, the terms emotional quotient (EQ) and emotional intelligence (EI) are often used interchangeably.[11]

Since then, the ongoing research of leading psychologists in the field of EQ—from the work of Goleman, John Mayer and Peter Salovey to that of TalentSmart and Multi-Health Systems—continues to prove the power of emotional intelligence. For example:

- In a study by Mark Slaski and Susan Cartwright, a high correlation was found between EI and overall managerial performance. A bonus? More emotionally intelligent managers seemed to experience less stress, be healthier, and enjoy their work more than those with less EI.[12]
- At a Fortune 100 insurance company, high-performing general agents were associated with 15 percent more growth than low-performing agents. Those high performers scored much higher in most areas of emotional intelligence than low performers.[13]
- In another compelling example, the U.S. Air Force was able to use emotional intelligence screening to increase by threefold their ability to hire successful recruiters, reduce first-year turnover rate, and reduce related financial losses by 92 percent.[14]

These are just some of the many studies that underscore the value of emotional intelligence in the workplace.

In the end, you don't have to understand every nook and cranny of EQ from a researcher's perspective to benefit from sharpening your own—instead, you need tools to help you leverage EQ. And that's what we'll do with the EQ tactics offered in this book—we'll focus less on the theoretical concept of EQ, as many business books already do this, and more on practical strategies for increasing your EQ and applying it in the workplace. That being said, this is a foundational chapter for everything to come, so let's make sure to get clear here on the difference between ego and EQ. Being able to slide on the spectrum away from ego toward EQ is one of the most effective approaches to maximizing your tenure at the top.

What's the Difference? Ego vs. EQ

For the purposes of this book, *ego* refers to that part of you that is concerned with the self. When properly balanced with EQ, ego can be an important pillar to success (in the form of self-confidence, assuredness, conviction, clear decision making, and more). Often in this book, however, we will be talking about the kind of ego that involves being *overly* concerned with oneself, to the exclusion of others—something we may be oblivious to even when we have the most noble intentions. This kind of ego, though sometimes helpful in *reaching* the top, can be a hindrance once you're there, ultimately sabotaging your success.

When a person is operating out of too much ego and not enough EQ, the person can become *egotistical*, showing self-involved behaviors and making comments that appear narrow in perspective. Then there's *egotism*, which the Merriam-Webster Dictionary defines as "an exaggerated sense of self-importance."[15] We can learn something, too, by looking at the synonyms for *egotistical*, including *arrogant*, *smug*, *conceited*, *self-centered*, *selfish*, and *narcissistic*. Those are all extreme adjectives, but still interesting to note: you start to get the picture when reading them. Too much ego isn't pretty and it isn't good for the organization.

Unfortunately, although most leaders don't want to be described as egotistical, their behavior may often be interpreted that way. *Undercover Boss,* the popular reality TV series on CBS, provides vivid examples of the common disconnect between the way leaders view themselves and the way their employees view them. When these business leaders go incognito in their own companies to find out what people on the front lines really think, the wake-up call they receive often catches them by surprise.

Now let's contrast ego with EQ. The following table shows a list of two kinds of statements (ego-based versus EQ-based), set side by side, to make the difference between ego and EQ clear.

TABLE 1: Ego-Based Statements vs. EQ-Based Statements

Ego		EQ
"I do things that are good for me."	vs.	"I put the needs of others before my own."
"I meet my needs first."	vs.	"I connect to what other people need from me."
"I expect everyone else to do the adjusting."	vs.	"I adjust to others even though that isn't always comfortable for me."

Clearly, there is a difference between these two kinds of statements: those on the left have a sharp emphasis on self; those on the right have a heavy emphasis on others. Both sides of the coin are extreme, so that operating exclusively out of one or the other (self versus other) can be problematic. For this reason, our conversation in this book will focus on identifying which of the common eight ego pitfalls may be invisibly hindering your effectiveness as a leader. In the process, we will reawaken the strong EQ skills you may have used to great effect in your earlier career days. (Interestingly, research has shown EQ to be highest in middle managers; it typically drops off as people rise through the ranks.)[16]

As a senior executive, business founder, or other leader, you are likely already very good at what you do. This is a book about becoming even better, by identifying your personal blind spots and by using the power of EQ to overcome them. I call it ego versus EQ: that dance between ego and emotional intelligence, that ever-important balancing act between self-confidence, outer strength, and superior technical expertise that helped you climb to your position today and the seemingly softer, more interior qualities of reflection, consideration, and connection that will ensure you stay there.

In addition to helping you get better at what you do, this book may also help you avoid the $6 billion mistake (or the 200-million-gallon oil spill). Why? Because here we can assess together the areas where top leaders have traditionally gone wrong and make sure you don't step in the same, pardon my French, dog poop.

Note: there *are* special instructions once you reach the top. Many of the business books out there today can help you refine your game as you climb to the pinnacle of your organization or business, but the special skill set you need to *stay* at the top has often been missing from the discussion. This book will give you a set of eight ego land mines to avoid and the respective EQ tactics that will help you recalibrate for success at the top—because the goal for many of us isn't just to reach the summit... it's to stay there.

It's a Hard Knock Life

It's tough being a CEO or business leader. Sure, you hold much of the power in the organization, and what *you* say ultimately goes. There's power in that. There's freedom! Yet the sober reality is that the numbers for long-term success are *not* working in your favor.

Here's a revealing snapshot that's hard to ignore.

- Two in five CEOs fail in their first eighteen months on the job, according to a study published by the *Harvard Business Review*.[17]

- One-third of Fortune 500 CEOs survive fewer than three years at the helm.[18]
- The majority of start-up businesses fail within five years, according to the Small Business Administration; two-thirds will disappear just a decade after founding.[19]

This prevalence of failure is not due to a lack of effort. For example, billions of dollars are poured annually into rolling out the latest and greatest technology, working with consultants to trim costs and boost profits, and training the workforce so they stay cutting-edge.

Yet the failure rate of CEOs and business owners isn't changing. News of CEO missteps, corporate oversights, and declines in profit still abounds. Why? The truth is that many of these initiatives and practices overlook the main influencer of the business's success: the executive leadership. Sure, there is often an ostensible focus within the company on sharpening leadership skills, particularly across the team, but how many CEOs and business owners are tuning in to the areas where they *themselves* are currently weak?

It's not easy to stay at the top of an organization—the numbers and the reality on the ground show that. There are market forces to deal with. Buyouts and takeovers. And let's not forget the ever-changing tastes of consumers, coupled with global and market fluctuations. All of these factors lead to legitimate business challenges. Yet some leaders manage to stay on top. It can't all be about external factors or just plain good luck. Successful leaders know how to balance their ego with a sharp EQ—awareness of the emotional context in which business takes place and an ability to respond to that context. With the help of the tools in this book and the keen new awareness that is likely to result, you can overcome your own ego blind spots with the engine of strong emotional intelligence powering you.

Avoid Overusing a Strengths-Based Approach

Undoubtedly, you bring many strengths to the table, strengths that have helped you rise to your current post as CEO, president, VP, chairperson, or other leadership position. Maybe it was your incredible technical expertise that brought you here, as was the case for Gary, mentioned earlier. Maybe it was your knack for knowing when to launch the new product that allowed you to get your division or business to take off. Or maybe it was your instinctive ability to detect risk and predict situations that ultimately helped you earn the title of successful business owner or CEO.

Whatever the strengths that brought you to this point in your career and business life, I want you to keep those with you. What's equally important, however, is to get a *full* picture of your strengths plus your weaknesses, so you can harness those strengths while working around any potential vulnerabilities. You want to ensure that your weak areas don't trip you up on your path to increased growth, higher returns, more reliable products, or any of the other goals you and the team may have set for the organization.

It's not always easy to hear, but we all have limitations—that's part of being human. Despite those individuals who take a strengths-based approach (i.e., rely on your "genius" and don't worry about your weaknesses), there are some real risks to senior leaders who choose to ignore their limitations or who don't understand or respond to them. Even the most self-aware, well-intentioned executive has to work hard to stay grounded. The air of success in the executive suite can get a little heady, clouding a leader's ability to view himself objectively. Compound that with the fact that the higher a person's rank, the less likely those around him are to give honest feedback. That can set a leader up for disaster at worst, dysfunction at best.

Think about it: if you are an individual at the top of the organization or business, those below you will not be inclined to give you criticism, even if it is constructive. Who wants to tell the boss she might be off base or the source of certain challenges within the organization? People may not want to risk the political fallout by giving honest feedback to the leader. That's strike one against you when it comes to understanding your weaknesses or limitations. Strike two? Maybe people have *tried* to give you feedback, only to see that you ultimately ignore it. So they stop. Possibly, strike three comes when people *do* give you feedback; you may make it so difficult that they don't want to risk your potential outbursts or defensive comments again.

As a result, it's easy to end up at the top of your organization with certain blind spots that fewer and fewer people are willing to call to your attention. Yet, sooner or later, those blind spots may cause you to stumble or drop the ball. I've already mentioned some egregious CEO blunders and could easily add others here. It might be tempting to think of Al Dunlap of Sunbeam, Bernie Madoff, or Jeffrey Skilling of Enron and throw them into the ego versus EQ pot. But not so fast. The majority of executives who fall into these traps are not on par with these notorious leaders. They are not bad people, and they are not egomaniacal or morally warped. They are hardworking, ambitious, and honest people who unintentionally get caught up in the dynamics and forces at play in the senior executive world. The ego traps explored in this book represent mistakes that all of us can make; the key is to keep your EQ sharp, which can help you to avoid making one of these blunders.

Eight Traps to Sidestep When Ruling the Mountaintop

Enough of this pessimism. You are likely an *A* player and are reading this book because you aim to continually get better at what you do. You realize that you can never take your position or your success for granted, and you're set on securing it. So as a starting point, let's take a look at the eight big ego traps, because even the strongest of leaders has the potential to fall into these from time to time. See if you recognize one or more of these traps, and start to gather the insight you may need to step your game up another notch. In future chapters, we'll go into greater depth on these, working to identify which few may represent your own Achilles heel. With that self-knowledge, you'll be prepared to explore the EQ antidotes for that particular ego trap and not only secure your own position at the top but ensure the success of your organization as well. Here they are:

- Ego Trap 1: Ignoring feedback you don't like
- Ego Trap 2: Believing your technical skills trump your leadership skills
- Ego Trap 3: Surrounding yourself with more of you
- Ego Trap 4: Not letting go of control
- Ego Trap 5: Being blind to your downstream impact
- Ego Trap 6: Underestimating how much you are being watched
- Ego Trap 7: Losing touch with the frontline experience
- Ego Trap 8: Relapsing back to your old ways

Each of these ego traps has its own flavor, and some of us are more prone to one than another. Occasionally, the ego traps pop up in combination with one another, which can lead to even more challenges for the leader and the team (more on that in the conclusion). These ego traps are everywhere. Take any CEO mistake and you can probably trace it to one or more of them—even for top leaders, like JP Morgan Chase's Jamie Dimon, who skillfully guided the bank through the difficult years leading up to the 2008 economic crisis and beyond. While other banks speculated and over-leveraged, Dimon balanced risks and stayed sufficiently conservative. Where other banks eventually faltered and collapsed, JP Morgan Chase emerged steady and strong. Yet, unfortunately for him and JP Morgan Chase, Dimon, too, may have eventually fallen into a few ego traps of his own, leading in some part to the company's later $6 billion loss.

Enter Ego Trap 1: According to a June 2012 *Businessweek* article, Dimon ignored feedback from other JP Morgan Chase executives who expressed worries about the dealings of the bank's CIO, under whose supervision the trading losses ultimately occurred.[20] In the same vein, Dimon was cited as having "rebuffed repeated warnings about the need to reduce...bets."

Also of note, Dimon's prepared statements for U.S. congressional hearings in June of 2012 indicated that he was "unaware of some of the risks that the bank's Chief Investment Office took when investing in risky derivative products that led to a $2 billion loss in May."[21] Did Dimon lose touch with his CIO, Irvin Goldman, and just as importantly, did Goldman lose touch with his traders? If so, Ego Trap 7—losing touch with the front line—may also have been at play. Dimon himself made the "stunning admission that the traders in London may have intentionally mismarked the trades to make them look less egregious."[22] One has to ask, what kind of pressure were these traders under that would cause them to mislabel trades? And did the CIO and Dimon understand that pressure, or had they lost touch with the day-to-day realities of the trading desk?

In all likelihood, it was a complex set of factors, combined, that led to the "London Whale" incident. But ego traps may certainly have been at play. Dimon was seen as a titan in the industry, which naturally could have set him up for the fall. As Gillian Tett notes in her book *Fool's Gold*, Dimon "was one of the few senior bankers who emerged...with a reputation that was not just intact, but soaring."[23] "We all bought into the idea that Jamie was the best manager in the world," says Paul Miller, a former examiner for the Federal Reserve Board of Philadelphia.[24] Chances are that Dimon *was* a good manager. He was one of the rare banking leaders pre-2009 who remained responsible in the company's hedging practices, enabling his bank to emerge from the economic crisis of 2008 unscathed, a rarity.

Yet perhaps it was *because* of Dimon's steadfast leadership that trouble eventually ensued. That is, when the CEO is sailing the corporate ship smoothly, there may appear to be less need for the hands on deck to step in with new directional advice (aka feedback), even when a storm is brewing. Add to that the fact that a confident, celebrated leader may not feel the need to listen as closely to feedback that *does* get shared. And then consider the added risk of surrounding oneself with all like-minded folks (as I will argue in the chapter on Ego Trap 3 this may have happened for Dimon), and warning smoke is even less likely to be sent up to the leader. As for Dimon, financial gurus, fellow bankers, and the U.S. government all gave him their seal of approval as a respected expert—why shouldn't he feel confident in his own decision making?

This is not about playing the blame game. Truth be told, these pitfalls are easy for even the most astute leaders to fall into. I'll be the first to confess that as CEO of my own company, I have stepped unwittingly into these ego traps over the years. I have found myself falling into Ego Trap 1, minimizing feedback about myself that is hard to hear (deflecting critical comments about my speaking events with statements like, "That audience was unique," "They specifically requested that topic so there was nothing I could do," "It was just one bad day, no biggie," etc.). And my team, who also wants me to succeed and not be hurt, chimes in, "Yes you are right, that was out of your control," thereby feeding my self-deception.

I can also make life tough for my support team because my communication style, combined with my personality traits, results in a lot of last-minute planning, which results in them having to quickly shift their own priorities and tasks at the eleventh hour (Ego Trap 5: being blind to the downstream impact of my behavior). Feeling bad about putting this burden on my administrative support team, I sometimes end up doing too much myself (Ego Trap 4: not letting go of control)—which only keeps the pressure on me, resulting in more last-minute planning. Get it? I make a living from recognizing the hallmarks of these traps, and it's still hard to maintain the self-awareness and self-discipline to avoid them.

That being said, I have discovered time and again myself—and when working with business leaders—that the effort invested in avoiding these ego traps and acting in a more emotionally connected way has both short- and long-term benefits. The payoff in my own work has been fewer errors, better-quality work (repeat speaking engagements because clients see me taking feedback and making improvements), and increased staff loyalty and retention (saving me hiring costs and training time).

As for my clients who have benefitted from identifying their ego traps and sharpening their EQ, I am reminded of a president who was named acting CEO, who hired an executive coach to keep him accountable. This CEO was concerned about the company's EBIT (profit), and instead of pointing fingers at his staff or at market conditions, he decided to look in the mirror. Realizing he needed perspective and a designated grounding voice, he hired a coach who helped him identify his blind spots, recognize his patterns for impulsive behavior, and learn strategies to ensure better execution among his senior team.

He has now made changes to the way he gives feedback and holds people accountable; he is also more aware of his influence—good and bad—on the executive team. Although he continues to actively refine his EQ, he began to see a marked difference after just ninety days. His people started taking him more seriously, staff meetings became more effective, and the organization is on track to have its biggest growth year in the company's history.

Another of my clients has seen her organization double in size since she took a long look in the mirror and not only became more mindful of her own ways but began to build an organization of emotionally savvy executives. Today she enjoys a retirement lifestyle because her organization is so self-sufficient. Whether it's deepened credibility with the executive team, renewed employee engagement, increased profits, or sharp gains in customer satisfaction, the benefits of sidestepping the ego traps in favor of emotionally intelligent leadership are tremendous. The many real-life stories to follow in this book will show both how and why.

In addition to sharing real anecdotes from the workplace, I cite research and respected publications to back up my points wherever possible. My intention with this book is to offer evidence-based advice—material that is grounded in what specialists in the field are finding to be true—so that you can trust that it's worth following. In fact, I hope to bridge a gap between the academic and the practical by providing you with useful tools that you can not only trust but can also use with ease at the office, in team meetings, on the road, and more. To that end, I offer a simple model in each chapter, which you can use to avoid the ego traps and engage your EQ at any time: *reading* your own emotions and moods at work (self-awareness), *recognizing* how others may feel in a certain situation (empathy), and *responding* with good judgment and consideration for the situation (self-control).[25]

By the end of this book, you will know the ins and outs of applying these elements of EQ in any situation, being able to use them reflexively in your best moments and turning to them for support when you find your stress level rising and your ego trying to sneak back in.

In a Nutshell

This book is not for everybody. If you have only experienced an upward trajectory of business success with no challenges over the course of your career, you may not want to bother reading it. If you have no personal shortcomings because you have already done a lot of self-analysis, make it a gift. But if you are like most of us, who face periodic workplace hiccups, occasional personnel problems, or perplexing relationship challenges at work, this book may be the perfect fit for you and your goals. If you are the type of leader who likes to look within, not just externally, when evaluating business challenges, read on. There is plenty waiting in these pages to help you step up your game—because there's always room for growth, even when you have made it to the top.

Then again, some of you may also be reading this book because you've had a recent wake-up call in the workplace. Maybe quarterly profits were sharply down. Maybe turnover has skyrocketed and your organization is bleeding talent. Or maybe you are curious about understanding your leadership effectiveness in ways measured beyond title, salary, or privileges. If you find yourself in any of these situations, this book is for you.

Whatever the reason, and no matter how good a leader you are, the ego versus EQ framework will invite you to look within. In the end, your own behavior is what you can control—not market conditions, not a board of directors, not a cataclysmic change in the industry. With so many factors *outside your control,* doesn't it make sense for you as a senior executive or business owner to ensure you are paying attention to what *is* within your control – *your own behaviors*? What shifts can you make in your behavior to safeguard against ego pitfalls that may await? What tactics can you employ to sharpen your EQ and reap its proven benefits? The good news: although there are eight common ego traps, most leaders fall into only a few of them. So you won't be asked to completely redesign who you are; instead, you'll be invited to make some small course corrections that will have a big impact.

To get the process started, we will follow the journey of other executives who only needed to do some fine-tuning to transform their leadership from good to amazing. Reading this book can help you open the door to identifying your own ego traps and can provide you with some simple actions to remedy them. Join me as we start this journey...

Ego Trap 1

Ignoring Feedback You Don't Like

When I am hired as a coach to work with an executive, I like to start our first meeting with a question that relates to the executive's effectiveness within the organization: *How are you doing as a leader?*

I want to know how the executive is doing, not as a technician or knowledge expert in his field, and not as an innovator or operations specialist, but as someone whose primary responsibility is to motivate others, create a common vision, and engage the workforce.

Most respond to my question with "Good...I think." Then they look at me with an expression that says, "What do you know that I don't know?" I want to smile and put them at ease because the truth is, I usually don't have any insider information. But I understand why they might think that I do. My question almost implies that there's a back-story. It feels like a setup. Plus, most executives already have a sense that something is just over their shoulder that they cannot see, waiting to bring down all their hard work.

No matter what the executive's answer, my next question is, "How do you know?" As in, "How do you know that your perception of your effectiveness as a leader is accurate?" Some leaders explain that they can tell based on their business results, and others are honest and say they really don't know that it is accurate—it's merely their gut sense. In most cases, though, it becomes clear to me that these executives may not have a full set of data points to help them assess their effectiveness.

Why does it matter whether you have an evidence-based report card of your leadership? Isn't leading others largely about feeling your way around the intangibles while focusing on hard-and-fast business results as your evidence of success? Many have tried this approach with varying degrees of success. What doesn't seem to vary in this approach is the lack of fulfillment from both leader and those being led—and the nagging feeling that there's more to this leadership thing than setting goals and measuring results.

To become a truly excellent leader who creates exceptional results, every executive or business owner needs to ask himself this question from time to time: "How am I doing as a leader and how do I know I have an accurate answer?" This all-important question should follow immediately: "How closely does my opinion of my performance match the opinion of my direct reports, my peers, and my boss?" The reality is that your success in leading others requires alignment between your self-perception and your followers' perception. From a leadership standpoint, it's an important distinction. The continuum runs from "plugged in" to "clueless." Where you fall on this scale affects not only your leadership credibility but your effectiveness and, ultimately, your career.

A useful tool for assessing whether there is a match between a leader's self-perception and the perception of others is the 360-degree feedback assessment—a survey taken by multiple people who work with the employee or leader, creating a full circle of feedback for that person. Ironically, in the majority of companies where my firm is called in by Human Resources to administer 360-degree feedback assessments, we are told to *exempt* the executives and/or business owners from the process. So at the same time that the executives want to know how employees are doing at an organizational level, they will often ignore the value of external feedback for themselves—an example of ego rearing its developmentally disruptive head.

In addition to sending a message of incongruent values to employees, this approach can help leaders continue unconstructive behaviors of which they may not be aware. What's more, the effort to get a read on everyone's performance becomes tainted because the leader is creating a contradiction between word and deed.

What leaders *do* is always more impactful than what leaders *say*. And, regardless of intent, the message to followers when leaders exempt themselves from the feedback process is clearly, "Do as I say, not as I do" or, worse, "I am okay, but you are not." My guess is that most leaders don't mean to make such statements. Yet when they forgo the feedback-gathering process for themselves, that's exactly what they are doing.

Forgoing Feedback Has Consequences

A study of thirty-nine thousand global leaders by PDI Ninth House confirms that there is, in fact, a significant correlation between an "inability or unwillingness to see one's own faults" and career stalling or derailment. Those who were identified as "out of touch" with the way their direct managers rated them were 629 percent more likely to "derail" (i.e., perform below the level of expected achievement, be demoted, or even be fired) than those who were in touch with the way their direct manager rated them.[1] Stop for a moment and reread that number…629 percent! That's a big, career-imploding difference. If that stat doesn't make you consider the importance of syncing your own assessment of your performance with the assessments of those around you—to gather and listen to feedback—what will?

There are a few reasons why executives and business owners may not include themselves in the evaluation process. Some leaders worry that they will be seen by their employees as vulnerable, weak, or flawed if they ask for feedback, as if it's a sign that they need help or are struggling with self-doubt. Others resist the discomfort of hearing potential criticisms about themselves because it can be painful or embarrassing. Or they have learned over the years that leadership is a perception game and they subconsciously avoid any risks to their self-image. Other leaders may believe that they are always open to feedback and are already doing their jobs really well, based on the positive comments they frequently get. As a result of this positive feedback (or sometimes simply a lack of negative feedback), this latter group of leaders ends up thinking that it's not necessary to gather formal feedback on themselves.

Regardless of the reason (all of them understandable), failing to solicit *developmental* feedback—or ignoring it when it's been given to you, while freely lapping up kudos—can have significant, negative consequences, whether in the form of weaker business results, lost credibility, wide-scale public criticism, or even job loss. An even subtler impact as a result of a feedback vacuum is the gradual erosion of credibility and influence, leaving a dedicated and tenured leader with little relevance or pull in the organization. When others see an executive as being self-contained and developmentally static, they often avoid meaningful interactions with the leader and create workarounds with others who demonstrate passion and connectedness. Insulating oneself from the risks of feedback doesn't provide safety; it simply exchanges temporary comfort for future instability. Cut yourself off from feedback sources and you nearly guarantee failure—often one you won't see coming.

Now let's talk about some bottom-line results. What the research tells us about high-performing leaders, according to the work of Allan Church, VP of Talent Management and Organization at Pepsico, and others, is that high-performing managers are *significantly more aware* of how their managers' view them than low-performing managers are.[2,3] Although we can't conclude that this awareness has *produced* high performance, we can't ignore the relationship either. After all, your boss is arguably your single most important stakeholder. If you are interested in emulating the behavior of other high-performing managers, you can't overemphasize the role of perceptions and adaptive self-awareness.

Self-awareness on the part of the leader also appears to be essential to success, as evidenced in a 2005–2008 study by Green Peak Partners and Cornell University. As noted in the introduction, self-awareness is a key indicator of emotional intelligence, which involves having a deep understanding of one's emotions, strengths, weaknesses, needs, and drives.[4] People with strong self-awareness are neither overly critical nor unrealistically hopeful. Instead, they are honest—with themselves and with others. In Green Peak's analysis of seventy-two senior executives across thirty-one companies, the researchers found that "a high self-awareness score was the strongest predictor of overall success."[5] The study was clear in showing that those executives who evidenced self-awareness were the same executives who were found to be doing a good job at driving results and managing talent.[6]

This research lines up with my experience in the workplace, where I have repeatedly seen that executives who demonstrate high self-awareness are also better able to share their reactions to information from employees, good or bad, without leaving people guessing as to what they really think. These same self-aware leaders do not take out a bad mood on someone else, and they tend to stay much more connected to what their followers really need from them. Perhaps more importantly, these leaders consciously, even if subtly, encourage and maintain relationships that provide them with holistic, high-quality business information.

What the studies by researchers like Church and Green Peak seem to be telling us, and what I and my colleagues are seeing, is that having multifaceted self-awareness is key. The ability to know yourself (what's called *emotional self-awareness*) and the ability to recognize how others see you (*social self-awareness*) both play a vital role in being an effective leader. You harness a powerful combination when you raise your self-awareness and then act on this new knowledge—it's like a secret recipe for engaging your followers and strengthening your own credibility. All this, just for taking an honest look in the mirror and making slight adjustments based on things you couldn't see before.

The High-Performing Leader, Defined

Of course, if you have reached the executive level, you must already be a high-performing leader. So, does it really matter how "self-aware" you are or how tuned in you are to feedback? I have plenty of executive and business owner clients who, at the beginning of our engagement, would argue that it does not. In fact, caring too much about what others think of them is considered a disadvantage rather than an advantage. In cases like these, my clients and I take some time to examine what it really means to be a high-performing leader, to show the gaps in this thinking.

Some of these leaders do well on business measures like revenue, market share, thru-put, earnings-per-share, or defect-free products—*functional* factors. It's in the other areas of their role as company *leader* that they may not be performing quite as effectively; these less tangible elements include motivating, managing, clarifying, and inspiring their team and employees. Red flags that these issues are occurring may show up in the form of high turnover, production problems, lack of innovation, or unionization by employees. When leadership breaks down in EQ-related areas, the other business functions get compromised too, even if it isn't always immediately evident. Sometimes the question has to be asked: Is there a secret cancer in your organization that you don't know about because no one's giving you the feedback you really need to hear?

No matter how "good" you feel your performance is or how great the company seems to be doing, the question remains: How much *better* might the company do if you added your own performance development as a leader to your business strategy? What are the opportunity costs of leadership blind spots? A high-performing leader, in the fullest sense, is able to not only create results but also to lead the individuals creating the results, amounting to an optimally successful organization.

In all of my work with executives, I have found the shared challenge of these highly intelligent, very talented leaders to be an inability to fully assess their own leadership effectiveness. Whether it is due to their own biases in evaluating their performance, the overall feedback vacuum that tends to exist at higher levels of the organization, or a difficulty in noticing or responding to the feedback that others are providing, *these leaders are often flying blind when it comes to assessing where they really stand.* That's Ego Trap 1, the first pitfall explored in this book because it represents such a pervasive and fundamental challenge for executives and business owners.

Happily, you can generate a road map for ratcheting up your leadership performance by simply gathering feedback. By regularly collecting, interpreting, and responding to feedback, you can become more self-aware, tuned in to your team, and effective in your role as company leader, motivator, and visionary. Gone will be that murky sense of "What don't I know?"—replaced with a clear understanding of how your people see you and what kind of a leader you truly are. It's not about inviting judgment *or* collecting accolades; it's about creating a crystal clear understanding of your strengths and weaknesses as a leader, information you can leverage, thus making it the ultimate secret weapon in the leadership game.

A Closer Look at the Trap

When it comes to Ego Trap 1, there are two main problems that typically occur. One is that the leader *does not formally invite feedback* from the team; the other is that the leader *ignores feedback* when it is provided. Let's look first at the case of not inviting feedback.

Failure to Solicit Feedback

It would be easy to think that only arrogant leaders don't bother to ask for feedback. In reality, it is often the most humble or beloved leaders who fall prey to this trap. Not because they don't care about employee feedback or don't want to hear it, but because they take the fact that their team is already close and is generally honest about big issues to mean that there is no need to formally invite feedback on their performance. They believe that their people will give honest performance feedback without being prompted or that they are doing so well that there's no need for a more formal evaluation. In other cases, they don't want to put individuals around them on the spot by asking their opinions on the company's leadership.

In a recent conversation I had with a CEO at a publicly traded national bank, I was asked directly about the value of gathering feedback. "Why do I need this?" the CEO asked with sincerity. "I have a great team that I have high trust in and an open dialogue with." He went on to explain that the group had worked together with him for a long time and had a high degree of candor. "So," he went on, "I hear feedback all the time." Then with a laugh, "Usually when people aren't happy!"

I felt for him. And he made a good point. Many executives say they hear feedback about their decisions quite often. It seems, though, that the feedback that most often makes its way up to the leader is vague, generic, or concerns the executive's policies or positions on issues rather than specific input on the leader's interpersonal effectiveness. I feared this CEO was in an even worse situation because, as I explained to him, it is usually the most well-respected CEOs who are at greatest risk of falling into this ego trap. Because a much-admired CEO's team likes and appreciates him, they don't want to hurt the leader's feelings. There may also be some unwritten cultural rules about who can deliver critical feedback up the food chain, what is acceptable behavior for a subordinate, or even what constitutes politeness at work. Because they think the leader is doing a good job overall, it's easier for the little criticisms to be minimized or ignored. Eventually, the feedback that was available is suppressed enough that the CEO is lulled into a false sense of security about his leadership performance.

In situations such as these, I encourage you as the leader to look at what *kind of feedback* the team has been giving you. Has it been related to your *effectiveness at motivating and engaging the workforce* or to things like satisfaction or dissatisfaction with the direction you are taking the company? Has it related to how effectively you are handling interpersonal relationships, or does it relate more to the way you have been handling deals or the more technical side of the job? Feedback on the latter aspects is fine, even useful, but it's also essential to regularly request and study feedback that relates to your ability to operate as a leader when it comes to "softer" skills like listening, approachability, and empathy.

Another challenge occurs in those cases where your team really does respect you so totally and completely that they have lost the ability to view your performance objectively. This is known as the "halo effect," a cognitive bias in which information that does not fit with the overall impression of a person is rejected. When individuals on your team are influenced by a halo effect, they will be operating on the premise that you are doing well overall and may be less primed to notice weaknesses that they could otherwise alert you to.

Daniel Goleman calls this dynamic the *CEO disease.* The problem, according to Goleman and his coauthors, is "an acute lack of feedback... Leaders have more trouble than anybody else when it comes to receiving candid feedback, particularly about how they're doing *as leaders...* the paradox, of course, is that the higher a leader's position in an organization, the more critically the leader needs that very feedback."[7]

A study by the Consortium for Research on Emotional Intelligence in Organizations confirms this need for feedback among those in the higher ranks. In studies examining more than a thousand employed individuals, the consortium showed that participants at the higher ranks (first-, mid-, and senior-level managers) had a significant pattern of rating themselves higher on their leadership performance than those around them rated them.[8] What's more, the higher a person's rank, the greater this gap became. These employees likely had higher levels of self-awareness when working at lower levels in their careers, but as they ascended the corporate ladder, the feedback faucet slowly closed.

It turns out the old adage about loneliness at the top may well be true—but it also appears to be self-inflicted. By using a process to actively solicit feedback from the team, these leaders could close this gap, gaining access to essential information that would help them refine their own performance and improve overall business outcomes.

Ignoring Feedback When It's Given

While some leaders are failing to formally gather feedback on their performance, others may fall into the trap of ignoring feedback when it's given. This can take the form of tuning out little cues that the team tries to provide; choosing, whether passively or purposefully, not to change in response to feedback when it's given; or outright refusing to listen. Regardless of the cause, the effect is the same.

Adriana, a second-generation Cuban American who had taken over her father's cigar business five years previously, fell into this last category.[9]

Adriana came to my attention after the company's board of directors called in my team. Adriana had repeatedly brushed aside suggestions from the director of Human Resources that she adjust her command-and-control leadership style, dismissing this advice even though the team had lost four members of the executive team within two years of her move to the CEO role. The director explained to Adriana in a private meeting, "The team is struggling with knowing how to work with you." Adriana's response was a curt and confident, "Too bad. If they don't like it, they can go work for another company."

From one perspective, Adriana's response was understandable. Her father and family had spent forty years building the cigar company from nothing after fleeing Cuba and settling in Miami in the early 1960s. They now made one of the most coveted cigar brands outside of Cuba. And there was no shortage of executive candidates interested in nabbing a top post at the company. Adriana herself was an intensely hard worker, at the office from six in the morning until eight at night most days, when she wasn't traveling to tobacco farms or manufacturing facilities. From the time she graduated from business school, Adriana had dedicated her entire life to the family business.

And yet if Adriana's goal was to make her family company as successful as it could be—not just maintaining her father's legacy but building on it—she could not do it alone. She would have to listen to the feedback being provided to her by the HR director as well as others on the executive team. The executive churn was taking a major toll on employee productivity and organizational morale, and was slowly eroding the company's reputation as an employer of choice. Ironically, by ignoring the needs of others Adriana was making her own goals and dreams unattainable.

Adriana has good company among executives and business owners, many of whom feel that it's not their job to respond to team or employee feedback. And because it is impossible to make everyone happy, there is a deep, dark secret of many CEOs, one that might be spoken only to an outside coach or mentor: "If they don't like the way the company is run, let them head for the door." Why *should* the CEO or leader be the one to do all the adjusting? Isn't the leader already doing so much?

There is no doubt that leaders are working very hard for their organizations. They are invested, they are dedicated, and they adjust regularly. The question is, is all that hard work and adjusting focused on the right areas? Feedback from the team offers an essential road map to where you as the leader can best put your energy. So it's not about becoming the ultimate accommodator; it's about you as the leader *not neglecting key indicators* that can help you sharpen business results.

This is not to say that every comment from every employee should be accepted at face value. The more responsibility you have, the fewer people there may be in your organization who truly understand your job well enough to deliver credible feedback. On the other hand, if a pattern emerges in what you hear, there may be some truths worth investigating. In addition, having trouble retaining people in positions that report directly to you may be a red flag warning you to stop and take a look in the mirror. A Gallup Poll of more than 1 million employed U.S. workers concluded that the number-one reason people quit their jobs is a bad boss or immediate supervisor.[10] Gallup also determined that poorly managed work groups are on average 50 percent less productive and 44 percent less profitable than well-managed groups.

The tricky thing is that even if you *want* the feedback from your people and even if you *ask* for it, once you rise to the upper ranks of the organization it can be very difficult to get objective feedback about your performance. Research shows that this issue of feedback (or lack thereof) at the upper levels of management is not simply speculation. As Goleman and his coauthors highlighted in their book *Primal Leadership*, a review of more than 175 studies looking at more than 28,000 managers indicated that "feedback on performance became less consistent the higher the manager's position or the more complex the manager's role."[11] In other words, the higher your rank as a leader, the more mixed messages you will probably get. What's more, negative feedback may come rolled up inside a compliment, or it may be given in layers of directness, with an employee easing into the worst after he sees how you respond to the easy stuff. If delivering bad news at your company is seen as risky or career limiting, the wheels will likely come off the feedback bus and all the passengers will get off and stay off out of self-preservation.

Once you're at the top, very rarely will anyone offer clear and direct feedback about your performance. You're going to have to listen for it, identify it, and actively invite it. And, to be honest, I don't believe asking for it yourself will get you feedback of any value. This is where outside resources come in, such as a leadership or executive coach, to help guide you through a structured process and help you create a framework of meaning from the data.

Culprits in the Feedback Vacuum

What makes it so difficult for leaders to receive feedback? There are a few reasons, one of which is on display in the story of Henri, the chief executive of a building products company. Henri is a dapper Frenchman who ran a successful company, and yet the business results started to stagnate. Quite admirably, Henri decided to make some changes, starting at the top—with himself. He hired me to help, with the goal of evaluating and improving his management style. I got the sense that his staff was a little surprised by the venture (as Henri had never been one to respond well to feedback) but was impressed by his willingness to look at himself from the get-go.

As we dove headfirst into a 360-degree assessment of Henri's leadership performance, he requested to have his executive team present to share his results. As we reviewed his feedback themes, I watched how the otherwise charming man lost all self-control and reacted defensively to every piece of constructive criticism. It was clear that his reaction was heartfelt and arose from the fact that Henri cared deeply about his reputation within the company. Still, rather than probe for more information or accept a comment quietly, he would question the veracity of every response and interject with a demand: "Am I really that way? Give me an example!"

The atmosphere in the conference room during the assessment review quickly grew tense. One manager summoned some strength and squeaked out, "Well, sometimes you seem a little unapproachable." Henri shot back: "I'm not unapproachable—no way. Give me an example of a time I wasn't approachable!" As the meeting wore on, the people who participated in the assessment spoke less and less, and the conversation went nowhere fast. I sat in the meeting, struggling with how to help the group get through to Henri, but eventually the feedback got so hard for him to hear that he walked out of the room abruptly. Several executives looked at me and threw their hands up in exasperation. I took a deep sigh. We certainly had some work ahead of us.

I contemplated what Henri's employees must have been thinking. If I reported to Henri and had sat in that 360-degree assessment meeting, how willing would I have been to give him my honest perspective on anything even slightly controversial, let alone my opinions about his lack of leadership? Not a chance. Who would? I was worried for Henri because I knew that in the future, when red flags popped up, few people would raise their concerns about his leadership style or decision making. In essence, Henri had dealt himself a crippling developmental blow from which he might not easily recover.

Despite his belief to the contrary, Henri did not make it easy for his team to share insights with him on how he was doing as commander in chief or how he could lead the company to greater innovation and success. In fact, quite the opposite. Becoming more effective as a leader— the very thing Henri was most passionate about and the reason he had sought out my firm—would be impossible unless he re-thought his approach to feedback.

Henri displayed raging defensiveness that made it challenging, if not impossible, for his team to give him honest, well-intentioned feedback. This was on full display at the 360-degree assessment meeting and had also been evident in previous interactions with his team. In addition, Henri's strong negative reaction to feedback rattled his team's confidence, making them wonder what Henri might do to them if they didn't back off. The contradiction, too, between what he said he wanted from them and his reaction in receiving it, also made the team question how much they could trust him. When trust and a sense of safety are at risk, performance plummets. Within a few years of our meeting that day, Henri quietly retired.

Whether the executive "feedback vacuum" gets created at your organization because you have a team who loves you and may not want to risk harming their relationship with you or because you've instead given your team signals that candid comments on your performance are not welcome, the rarified air at the top—devoid of feedback—can leave you uninformed and vulnerable on important performance issues, resulting in unexpected consequences and unpleasant surprises.

YOU KNOW YOU'VE FALLEN INTO EGO TRAP 1 IF . . .

- You take the fact that you don't receive much negative or constructive feedback as a sign that you are doing your job as a leader really well and don't need to focus on your own leadership development.
- You assume, without testing, that if your team is honest with you about operational issues that they can also be relied upon to give you candid feedback about how you are doing as a leader.
- You do not regularly ask your team for feedback, and when people attempt to give you some form of feedback, you rebuff or ignore them rather than inviting them to share more.
- You think secretly to yourself: "If they don't like what I'm doing, they can go get a job somewhere else!"

The Battle of Ego vs. EQ

It's not too difficult to connect the dots and see the role ego plays in the trap of ignoring or failing to gather feedback from others. At the heart of this challenge is a leaders' potential to overvalue their *self*-assessment while failing to check in with *others'* assessments of their performance.

Arrogance is not necessarily what triggers this ego trap. While there are certainly executives with overinflated egos who feel they are so spectacular in their leadership that they don't need to ask others how they're doing, more often, the leaders just don't remember to step outside their own mind-set to check in with others about their perspective. It's easy to do. Executives often maintain a breakneck pace and they may not have stopped to take stock in a long while, if ever. So it's common for those in high-level management positions to lose touch with the way that others view their performance, and even over inflate it. In the absence of credible information to the contrary, who doesn't want to believe their own good press?

While the ego tells leaders that this lack of constructive feedback is a sign that they are doing "great," EQ reminds leaders to stay grounded in what's true by soliciting feedback from others and using that feedback to create a more complete picture of their performance. A healthy dose of regular feedback from others can help keep the ego in check and allow the benefits of EQ to flow. Remember that ego and EQ are mutually exclusive: you must make a conscious and daily choice about which one will dominate your conduct.

The EQ–Feedback Loop

The idea of gathering feedback may sound daunting, unappealing, or messy. Will it lead to a flood of comments and critiques that just keep on coming? Will it upset the power balance between you and your team? Will the group now see you as weak or struggling? Many leaders worry this will be the case, when in fact, the opposite is usually true. Team members respect and appreciate the humility that comes with a leader asking for feedback—as well as the opportunity to provide their own valuable insight to help the whole team and organization run better. The trick is figuring out how to gather that feedback, understand the patterns and themes, and respond to it effectively.

Research from the Hay Group (a leading EI research and assessment firm) reveals that people who really improve their EQ are feedback junkies. According to the Hay Group, these individuals "are tenacious about asking those around them for feedback to see if they're doing well." My own experience coaching leaders confirms that, after the initial sting of hearing honest criticism wears off, most senior executives ask for more feedback. Once they have it, they start to use it as a key indicator for how they should execute their overall business strategy.

Feedback provides leaders with valuable input on how to ramp up their EQ in several key areas:

- Recognizing their own impulses before acting on them (self-awareness)
- Relating better to others, meeting their needs when appropriate (empathy)
- Moderating their own behavior (self-control) to avoid unproductive interactions and responses

The EQ competency is made up of several skills, and, as I mentioned in the introduction, self-awareness, empathy, and self-control are the vital three, the key trilogy of emotional intelligence that will be encouraged throughout this book. Gathering feedback is fundamental to keeping your EQ strong in these areas and to avoiding the ego traps. It's for this reason that *ignoring feedback you don't like* is the first trap discussed in this book. The following example shows the value of listening to feedback.

The Benefits of Feedback, in Action

Anthony, Dan, and Monica, managing partners at a West Coast financial services firm, decided to include themselves in the organization's 360-degree feedback assessments. Through this process, the three partners discovered that all were very weak at delegating decisions. The partners' first reaction to this feedback was to discount it, saying, "We delegate decisions all the time. We don't know what they are talking about!"

After additional digging and discussion with me, however, the problem became clear. Although the partners would say to the team, "This decision is yours to make," the unspoken message was "...but don't screw this up and be sure to run it by us before you spend any money." When the team checked in with the partners about a decision, they would often suggest changes, show disappointment in the decision, or add new information, eventually pressuring the employees to backtrack and let the partners make the decision themselves. While the partners preserved for themselves the illusion that they were delegating, their behavior actually belittled the team's efforts and made them less inclined to put much work into making a decision, knowing it would likely be overruled anyway. That situation was lose–lose for everyone.

After eventually accepting and reflecting on the feedback, the partners at the firm came up with a plan for improving the situation. They became clearer about times when they simply wanted *recommendations* from the team versus times when it was appropriate for the team to make decisions themselves, like the choice of coffee vendor to supply the break room. For high-impact decisions, such as whom to hire, a decision-making committee with full authority to hire was created. This gave the partners comfort that all hiring decisions would be carefully considered before offers went out, while at the same time keeping their own hands out of the pot.

In addition to making these specific adjustments, the partners could take this new understanding and apply it broadly going forward. Even though it was uncomfortable at first, they became better able, on the spot, to recognize moments when they were tempted to take decision-making authority away from an employee. They learned to moderate that impulse and choose a more productive behavior, like asking employees to share more of their logic for recommending a certain decision or suggesting that they take the decision to the committee that had been set up.

Since the three partners have initiated this program of annual 360-degree feedback assessments, their success has been astounding. Assets under management have grown tremendously, by $4 billion in one particular year. The partners' commitment to taking responsibility for developing their own performance in response to feedback likely played a significant role in that growth.

EQ Antidote: Recognizing, Reading, and Responding

So what's the clever solution to avoiding Ego Trap 1? I recommend creating a mechanism within your organization by which you will regularly receive feedback. Admittedly, this solution is more straightforward than clever, but it does get the job done. And what busy leader doesn't appreciate a little efficiency?

As I mentioned when I discussed Henri's situation, the vehicle I most recommend is an annual 360-degree feedback assessment, which can be implemented either formally or informally. The 360-degree feedback assessment is an instrument commonly used at respected institutions like the Harvard Business School, The Center for Creative Leadership, and Covey Leadership. It is a tool that generates an objective picture of a leader's performance on key emotional intelligence indicators, such as teamwork and collaboration, conflict management, transparency, emotional self-control, and adaptability via a multi-rater survey. If you have never taken a 360, I strongly encourage you to, *especially* if your employees are being asked to do it. And don't worry, you aren't required to share your results with anyone.

The 360-Degree Feedback Assessment at a Glance

A formal 360-degree feedback assessment typically involves an online survey that is taken by you as well as by a group of individuals who are likely to have a solid read on your performance—peers, direct reports, a manager if you have one, and even clients or outside people who interact with you on a regular basis. During the process, you will provide answers to an online assessment, as will these other individuals, and will receive a formal, written report that provides you with a quantifiable gauge on your effectiveness as a leader.

Like the formal 360-degree assessment, the *informal version* helps outline a full circle of feedback on your performance from those around you, except that the informal feedback is gathered via in-person or phone interviews by an objective person rather than through online survey responses.

As you learn more about each of these approaches, you can select whichever one you feel best fits your situation, needs, and organization. Another option to consider is implementing both the formal and informal 360-degree assessment, as many of my clients choose to do. Together, they provide you with both qualitative and quantitative data that can offer rich insight and measurement of your performance as a leader.

Note that a key aspect of the 360-degree assessment (whether formal or informal) is the involvement of a qualified executive coach. The role of the coach is to make it easier for your team to be candid in their comments, as well as to help *you* sort through which feedback to focus on and which feedback is okay to set aside.

Most 360-degree feedback assessments come at reasonable cost ($500 to $1,000) and can be done in a few weeks. The cost is negligible given the invaluable information you're likely to gain—on areas where you're doing well as a leader as well as those where you could stand to make some adjustments. For example, you may receive high praise for your ability to manage conflict while discovering that your team finds you abysmal at leading change. Or you may be surprised to find that your efforts to make lighthearted small talk with the group have been misconstrued because of bad timing or poor choice of setting, while the few times you stopped and asked individual employees how they were doing at home and at work had a positive impact.

With the 360-degree findings at your disposal, that vague question, "What aren't my people telling me?" can dissipate because you now have many of the key answers that were previously left unsaid. Instead of playing at the guessing game, trying to make the right changes when you sense discontent or hear grumblings from the team, you now have a clear road map for change—compiled based on quantitative and qualitative input and the guidance of an expert coach dedicated to helping you fulfill your potential as a leader. When I administer the 360-degree feedback assessment for my clients, I like to think of it as a powerful secret weapon that will give them an edge over leaders at competing organizations. Why? Because executives and business owners who are willing to make meaningful change in their behavior based on data have a whole new means of helping the organization run optimally, and it's a tool that I guarantee many other leaders have overlooked.

Turning the Feedback Picture into Actionable Advice

Seeking out feedback can open the door to a new understanding of how to improve your performance. The next question might be: How do you operationalize the feedback once you receive it? The three Rs of recognizing, reading, and responding offer an EQ prescription for success.

To begin, you can use the feedback provided by your team as a tool for *recognizing* how you are perceived by others. Think of it as a peek into what other people are saying about you when you're not around. Once you work through the feedback—and any emotional or defensive reactions it may understandably generate in you—with your coach, you can use the information to create a more complete understanding of your current effectiveness as a leader (that's self-awareness, in EQ terms).

With this self-awareness at the ready, you'll be primed to *read* and process the feedback cues that people give you on a day-to-day basis. While the 360-degree assessment typically provides you with a once-a-year opportunity to see how others are viewing your performance, it's also important to tune in to any spontaneous, informal feedback that your team gives you throughout the year—that's where reading comes in, and you'll have to be astute to accomplish this.

Much of the time, daily feedback will be delivered to you in vague terms, tied to business issues or masked within praise so as not to hurt your feelings, or, more often, so the employee does not to have to deal with your reaction. So you'll need to listen for the cues and really observe what people are trying to communicate to you. Is someone looking nervous while talking to you about the way a recent meeting went? Does a colleague seem hesitant to respond when you are venting to him about another team member? On the flip side, when someone is giving you praise, is she also embedding a constructive request for change within it? If someone looks uncomfortable or hesitant while telling you something, a little red flag should pop up, encouraging you to tune in and ask more. You can also look for common themes among statements by your team members and use these as valuable clues on where your people may need you to adjust.

The last piece of the EQ antidote is to *respond* in an emotionally intelligent way to any valuable feedback you receive. This might mean exercising self-control in situations where you would previously have reacted differently, using empathy to guide a useful, others-directed response. So if a team member comes to you confessing that he made an error on a recent financial report, you might resist the urge to immediately reprimand him as you would have done in the past and ask instead with sincerity, "What do you think happened here?" If one of your VPs shows up late for a meeting, you might choose to avoid embarrassing her in front of the group and realize that everyone has moments when she needs to be cut some slack. If it's a pattern with the VP, you may choose to have a private conversation instead of making the issue public.

Regardless of the specifics, the EQ prescription for Ego Trap 1 has you recognizing your own impulses (e.g., resisting the urge to interrupt others while they are speaking), reading how the other person may feel about or perceive the situation (concerned, excited, worried), and responding in a way that builds trust and morale. Ultimately, the feedback that you and your executive coach curate can provide you with a clear readout of the areas where you can best spend your energy developing your leadership performance, while the three Rs of recognizing, reading, and responding can offer the formula for how to execute.

FIVE TIPS FOR HANDLING THE FEEDBACK PROCESS

1. Don't look at the 360-degree feedback as an isolated data point. Plan to have someone who can help you make sense of the feedback, figure out the themes in the feedback, and decide what you should be spending your energy on in the near term.
2. Remember the good news about EQ—it is learnable. EQ skills can increase with focused effort.
3. Avoid becoming so feedback-sensitive that you react to everything that others say about you.
4. Focus on changing just one or two things based on what you hear. Small adjustments to high-impact areas can make a big difference in your effectiveness. And consider checking back with the person who was nice enough to deliver the feedback in the first place to ask how you're doing. It says you appreciate their input, which means they're more likely to help in the future.
5. All of us have blind spots. It is better to know what people think so you can do something about it. Remember, too, that feedback is hard to deliver. It's much easier to let you continue doing what you are doing, so when you do get feedback, treat it as a gift.

In a Nutshell

In organizations throughout the world, consultants are being brought in to administer evaluations of employees' performance. Too often, however, the top leadership exempts itself from these valuable opportunities for feedback. Unfortunately, these are missed opportunities that cannot be replicated elsewhere.

It's just too hard, without this evaluation process, for leaders to get the honest feedback that they need to do a good job running the team. Once at the top, there are *fewer opportunities* for leaders to receive feedback (without leadership above them to provide it), and peers and direct reports are typically *far less inclined* to give feedback. When these individuals do step up, they may not be direct in their critiques, making it easy for the leader to overlook the feedback or to ignore it altogether.

Regardless of the reason, if you are not actively seeking feedback from your team and/or are not hearing and responding to it when they provide it, you are stepping into Ego Trap 1. It's a case of believing that your own self-assessment is enough to guide you (ego alert!) while not appreciating the necessity of understanding other people's perspectives (EQ needed!). This approach can rob you of a precious opportunity to improve your own performance, that of your team as they begin to respond to your further development as a leader, and that of your organization. The solution? Annual 360-degree assessments and daily listening for and responding to feedback lead to a win–win approach that gets easier over time and leads to a continuous cycle of growth for everyone.

By grounding yourself in the stories that others tell about you as a leader, you gain the humility and awareness needed to reshape those stories. You become the *informed* author of your own story of leadership—smarter, wiser, and more connected to your team. The result? A powerful opportunity for transformation into the leader you *really* want to be and the leader your people and organization truly need.

APPLYING THE THREE R'S

Recognize your own first defensive impulse (self-awareness) when you are given feedback by asking questions in the moment or scheduling a follow-up meeting for a time when you're feeling more in control. Buy time to process the feedback internally by gathering additional information, and don't necessarily take everything at face value. Ask open-ended questions that help round out what the person is trying to tell you.

Read the person's comfort level. Appreciate how hard it is for the person to give you feedback and don't dismiss what the person has to say; acknowledge the validity of his perspective and experience (empathy). Read how the person is reacting to your body language and comments during the conversation. Does the person relax and share more feedback as the process unfolds, or does she shut down and back off?

Respond by thanking the person for sharing her feedback with you and acknowledge that it probably wasn't easy (self-control). Admit that everyone has blind spots. When the impact of your behavior was negative, let the person know that was never your intention. Explain that you need time to process the feedback, listen to other sources who may feel the same, and determine the best way to make changes.

Ego Trap 2

Believing Your Technical Skills Trump Your Leadership Skills

Every organization needs a genius—someone who is so well versed in her field or so adept at her craft that she can serve as the ultimate go-to person in the company. Having a superstar leader at the helm can result in a company with innovative products, a keen sense of what the market needs now and next, or exceptional customer loyalty. For Apple that genius was Steve Jobs; for Microsoft it was Bill Gates. At GE it was Jack Welch; at Facebook it's Mark Zuckerberg. At your organization, it may be you!

For a large regional insurance company that I was called in to support, it was Gary, a legal genius who could cite case law at a moment's notice, dismantle even the best argument, and negotiate winning contracts for the company. An intense man with a sharp sense of humor, Gary was a good example of a senior executive with incredible technical expertise. Not only did he have a vast cache of knowledge to draw from at a moment's notice, he had a shrewd debating style that made opposing counsel fear him. Everyone wanted Gary on his side of a legal challenge, as he was often the brightest legal mind in the room. Now, did that also mean everyone wanted Gary as the leader of his team? That was another question altogether.

Over the years, Gary had been promoted into leadership posts because of his incredible technical skills and expertise. Gary was given responsibility for supervising a legal department. While continuing to balance his own workload—filing responses, reviewing claims, and protecting the company in other ways—Gary also had to supervise other attorneys, delegate tasks to paralegals, and hold weekly staff meetings, all duties that come with leadership. Unfortunately, it quickly became clear to everyone that Gary was struggling with his new role. That is, it was clear to everyone except Gary. By the time I interviewed them, team members described Gary as "arrogant, condescending, and dismissive." They complained that he lacked basic people skills. He was constantly interrupting individuals who were in the middle of talking, waving them off from his doorway when he didn't feel like being interrupted, and even picking up the phone in the middle of a conversation with someone so that he could make an unrelated call. As for the combative style that Gary used so handily in legal situations? Well, he took that right into team meetings where the goal should have been working together, not forcing sides.

Even so, Gary's talents and expertise as an attorney seemed to win out—for the short term. And why not? Nothing he did or didn't do from a people-management standpoint diminished his reputation as the best legal representative the company could have. He got promoted again and again. People were willing to let Gary slide on the finer points of emotional intelligence because he was *so good* at what he did as a lawyer. They respected his genius and tolerated his boneheadedness. In spite of his interpersonal flaws, Gary's subject-matter expertise remained highly valued by the organization. In fact, management would regularly pat Gary on the back for his work, telling him how amazing he was and asking, "What would we do without you?" You can imagine the eye-rolling by any of Gary's employees who were within earshot of the accolades.

For his part, as far as Gary knew, he was a Legal Superman. Although management silently disapproved of the way he interacted with his teams, they gave no indication to Gary that working on other aspects of his leadership responsibilities was a critical activity for him to worry about. Instead, they tried to appease employee complaints, drawing attention to the fact that Gary was a crucial asset to the organization and brought success to them all. So Gary didn't bother paying attention to his interpersonal behavior. He had taken a classic fall into Ego Trap 2, believing that his expertise and talent as a lawyer were far more important than his "people" skills—even worse, because he believed that his technical skill excused him from relating to his people altogether.

Ego Trap 2 gets triggered any time a leader overvalues his technical skills, industry knowledge, or field expertise at the expense of other emotionally intelligent leadership attributes, such as flexibility, self-control, and social skill. Sometimes this plays out to the extreme with an executive like Gary, who borders on the conceited. Gary's attitude went something like this: "I'm a brilliant lawyer who gets the job done and that's what counts. To heck with complaints that I'm not nice enough. If you want nice, you go to Grandma's house. If you want expert legal leadership you come to me." Unfortunately, while Gary had the legal piece down, he was a complete amateur when it came to leadership skills.

At other times Ego Trap 2 gets triggered for leaders who are far less arrogant than Gary, but for whom technical expertise is a safe zone where they are comfortable playing. Leadership skills just don't come naturally for this group, or they seem too time consuming or complicated to learn, so avoidance sets in. Either way, Ego Trap 2 can be a deal breaker for executives who are trying to stick their landings at the top after being promoted there. For business owners, Ego Trap 2 is just as salient an issue, given that these leaders have often built successful companies on their high proficiency as experts in their fields. Business owners will often defend their EQ defects (as Steve Jobs did) by pointing to their entrepreneurial success, yet the reality is that EQ is an essential piece of the leadership pie.

A Closer Look at the Trap

At organizations across the country and around the globe, employees are being promoted into the leadership ranks because of their expertise in their *functional work area*, not necessarily due to their strengths leading people. Do any of the following sound familiar?

- The lead sales rep gets promoted to regional sales manager because of her great talent for wooing clients.
- The best programmer gets tapped to run the software development department, even though he rarely looks up from the computer or talks to people.
- The clinical research assistant is moved into the clinical development manager role because her projects come in on budget and on deadline, though she leaves a wake of people feeling bullied and coerced.

In many cases, the person who is best at doing sales, programming, research, marketing, and so on gets appointed to be the executive for that area of the organization. And I agree that promotions should be based on excellent performance, yet in leadership roles, technical expertise in one's field is never enough.

Technical vs. Leadership Skills

A recent analysis in the *Harvard Business Review* confirms that technical skills alone can't make the leader. After assessing hundreds of executive profiles, authors Boris Groysberg, L. Kevin Kelly, and Bryan MacDonald noted that they had discovered "one strikingly consistent finding: Once people reach the C-suite (the level of Chief X Officer), technical and functional expertise matters less than leadership skills and a strong grasp of business fundamentals....the skills that help you climb to the top won't suffice once you get there."[1]

Sometimes executives need fundamental relationship skills that are simply outside their scope of traditional expertise and are not taught in business school. The demands of today's economy and marketplace call for leaders to be able to cross outside of their traditional role as field expert into the realm of strong business leader. The EQ-based talents, such as being able to motivate team members, get buy-in, and lead change, are the real leadership deal makers.

Gary, our legal genius, was a great example: although he could spot wording snafus in a legal document from a mile away, he was perfectly miserable at motivating his team to excel and getting them invested in proposed initiatives. Instead, he regularly crushed morale with his gruff and pompous style—one minute shooing others away from him, the next holding them captive as he showed off his legal superiority. While Gary had been promoted to chief legal officer based on his legal acumen, it was becoming ever clearer that his expertise in the law would not be enough to keep him there. That is, if the company didn't want to lose everyone on the team except Gary.

It's not really fair to blame leaders like Gary for overvaluing their technical skills, as this approach seems endemic in many organizations. As management consultant Mark Murphy, CEO of Leadership IQ, put it, after studying 5,247 hiring managers from 312 companies, he's concluded that the average job interview focuses on making sure:

> ...that new hires are technically competent, but coachability, emotional intelligence, motivation and temperament are much more predictive of a new hire's success or failure. Do technical skills really matter if the employee isn't open to improving, alienates their coworkers, lacks drive and has the wrong personality for the job?[2]

In fact, findings in Murphy's 2005 study (which looked at twenty thousand new hires) confirmed that a lack of EQ skills were far more related to failure in a position than were lack of technical skills. Those who did not succeed in their new posts had failed largely because they couldn't accept feedback (26 percent), they were unable to understand and manage emotions (23 percent), they lacked the necessary motivation to succeed (17 percent), or they simply had the wrong temperament for the job (15 percent).

The first three relate directly to EQ, indicating that 66 percent of new hires failed because of issues related to low emotional intelligence, and I would argue the last is peripherally related to EQ as well, since higher self-awareness leads to choosing more suitable work environments. As for technical skills, only 11 percent of the new hires failed because of a deficiency in this area. As I sometimes hear, technical skills may get you in the door, but EQ skills determine whether you stay.

Why Are Technical Skills Overvalued?

Why is it that leaders like Gary fall so hard into Ego Trap 2, thinking that technical expertise outweighs the need for leadership skills? There are a few reasons. For starters, many organizational cultures encourage this misstep (as we've discussed) by hiring and promoting based on the technical skill set, and even overdoing the praise ("Gary, what would we do without you?"), while putting little emphasis on development of people skills. The technically savvy executive in turn fails to value leadership responsibilities, and figures, "If the company values me for being a technical genius, then that's enough." It's a fair reaction. Employees are often conditioned to pay attention to what the company values and rewards, and if no light hits the blind spot, it remains hidden. If there are no clues that leadership skills are equally valued, there is no reason to leave the functional comfort zone.

Another common source of the problem is that these EQ-based leadership skills sometimes don't come naturally, and resources on how to develop these capacities are not readily available or easy to grasp.[3] Further complicating the situation, the leader may *lack awareness* that, once he's in a top post, the game really does change. Skills and habits that worked in the past—even led to success and accolades—may no longer be needed or appropriate at the executive level (think back to Gary's interrogative style). So the very work style and strengths that initially help some leaders advance to the top echelons of the company may become a hindrance once they arrive. Trouble ensues when the leader doesn't realize the need for new learning or the value of a different approach.

This was the case for Tanya, a highly skilled player in her company's Human Resources department. Tanya started as a frontline manager for the organization and received multiple promotions along the way. Eventually, she was tapped for an assignment as interim executive vice president of Global Human Resources (after two people above her vacated their positions). A smart, soft-spoken woman who dressed and acted conservatively, Tanya was a quiet doer who was recognized by her organization as extremely skilled in her field. She could always be relied upon to interpret leave policies, understand compensation strategies, and put together relocation packages. Her attention to detail was superb, highly valued in a field where potentially costly agreements between the organization and employees were regularly negotiated. So where did Tanya go wrong?

Like Gary, Tanya had been continually promoted based on her ability to get things done in her area of expertise. It was not arrogance about her expertise that got in the way of Tanya leading her team once she became the acting global leader of the group. Instead, it was a lack of understanding that *her technical skills were not enough to make her successful in her new role*. In fact, the very skills that got Tanya promoted would, without EQ to balance them, turn out to be harmful. (Yes, even HR people can have low EQ.)

As each new leadership opportunity arose, Tanya neglected to read the needs of the situation and instead relied solely on her technically competent by-the-book brain. She regularly missed clues in front of her and lacked the situational awareness required to *feel her way* through decisions. The result? She defaulted to using her technical skills, which she had long relied upon and had been highly praised for in the past. Unfortunately, this approach ultimately sabotaged Tanya's ability to lead, influence, and inspire others.

For example, when attending an important employee meeting that involved multiple big players and a hot topic of discussion, Tanya completely misread her role and the environment. Instead of taking a leading role in the discussion, she offered to take notes, as the group watched in disbelief. Tanya's credibility as global leader was immediately diminished as she shifted into an administrative role, a blast from her past and, compared to the skills required in her new job, a retreat into her comfort zone.

In an instance of emotional detachment, Tanya led Kim, a veteran employee who had opted to take an early retirement package, through her exit interview. Tanya coldly denied the woman's sentimental request to keep her company badge, which had her photo on it from her first day of work twenty-five years earlier. Imagine how heartbroken and stunned this dedicated employee must have felt when her leavetaking was treated like a mere transaction. Then imagine how quickly everyone Kim worked with learned of, and reacted to, her treatment. HR's reputation, and by extension, the organization's reputation, took a profound hit that day.

Because Tanya was still doing double duty as global head and functional support to her internal client groups, she had to juggle the player–coach role. This made it all too easy to fall into Ego Trap 2—to rely on her technical skills as HR expert ("badge, please") rather than applying the emotional intelligence of a skilled leader and considering the employee's request. Tanya stepped headlong into Ego Trap 2, clinging to her hard skills as a field expert instead of shifting into a new way of interacting as an executive leader, one who possesses the power of discernment in decision making.

Ego Trap 2 is an easy one to get triggered for leaders. For business owners, who have founded their companies on their own smarts and technical gifts, it can also be hard to imagine that their technical proficiency might get in the way of their leadership. Yet when a leader continues to grind out responses to team members in the role of the "expert" rather than taking on the mantle of chief motivating officer, that technical prowess can become an albatross.

The trick is to know:

- When to leverage your technical expertise and when to keep it under wraps
- How to encourage your team to develop confidence in their own technical skills, and not have to be the smartest person in the room
- How to adjust to the needs of your followers instead of working in your comfort zone and expecting everyone else to always do the adjusting to you
- When to fix or get involved and when to purposely stay on the sidelines so others can learn and shine

Each of these skills involves being able to balance your own natural ego response with the needs of other team members, along with reading the context of a given situation. That's where EQ offers us an essential road map.

YOU KNOW YOU'VE FALLEN INTO EGO TRAP 2 IF . . .

- You consider being a subject-matter expert enough to make you a great leader and feel this excuses you from wasting your time accommodating people.
- You listen in meetings for chances to jump in and share your expertise or catch others in a mistake rather than letting them work

through the issue at their own pace and honoring their process, knowledge, and creativity.

- You take great pride in having been told by others that you are a "genius" at what you do while ignoring or minimizing feedback that you could improve at some of the "softer" leadership skills like listening, empowerment, or communication skills.
- You think being a leader means being the "fixer."

The Battle of Ego vs. EQ

Avoiding Trap 2 demands an ability to moderate ego with a healthy dose of EQ. It's a shift from an attitude of "I'm highly skilled in my field and that's what matters" to "My technical skills form my foundation as a leader; now my job is to help bring out that expertise in my people." Rather than asking, "How do I demonstrate that I have the expertise that merits me being here?" you now must ask, "How can I use my expertise to support my team and enhance their success?" There's a setting aside of self that happens when you slide from ego toward EQ and fully step into the role of leader.

Not all egotistical behaviors are represented by blowhards like Gary. As we have seen with Tanya, sometimes Ego Trap 2 is subtle and represents a self-centeredness that appears to others as detachment or obliviousness. Ego in this context refers to the gut reflex to react from one's own well-worn impulses without understanding, or even considering, others' needs or moderating one's own behavior to accommodate a given situation. That's where EQ comes in: that capacity to tune in to oneself (rather than reacting before tuning in), as well as the ability to tune in to others, and then respond accordingly.

Think of Tanya and the departing veteran employee, Kim, who asked to keep her company badge for old time's sake. HR expert Tanya, with years of experience conducting exit interviews and a razor-sharp memory for company policy, had a simple, gut response to Kim's request to keep the badge: "Sorry, it's company policy to collect ID badges—for security reasons." Kim, feeling a bit sad and sentimental about retiring, experiences a metaphoric slap in the face as the highest-ranking HR person—the very woman who should have the power to make exceptions to company policy—makes no effort to accommodate Kim's special and perfectly understandable request. Tanya's ego wins in that round, while her potential for EQ gets trampled.

What would have happened, however, if Tanya had possessed the EQ skills to observe herself (tune in to her egoistic impulses) before reacting? What if she had also been aware of her own temptation to default to her role as technical expert rather than stepping up as an interpersonally savvy leader? Tanya would have had a whole range of possible alternate responses at her disposal (deactivate the sensor, extract the photo, make a photocopy, etc.). Regardless of the specifics, a simple statement from Tanya, such as, "I realize that this is important to you, let me see what I can do," would have gone a long way toward maintaining the relationship with Kim and would have avoided diminishing the morale of other employees when word got out. (And yes, it spread like wildfire.)

Instead, Tanya stuck to her guns, true to her transactional framework, and retrieved the badge; the story quickly leaked into the company lunchroom and she was renamed "Badge-zilla." Sadly, no one wanted to tell Tanya directly about this growing reputation, and eventually the decision was made to remove her from her post. I met with her for the first time within a few weeks of the announcement, and she said it came as quite a surprise to her. I could see how hard it was for her to understand. She was caught off-guard and felt hurt and disappointed that no one had given her the feedback directly, and *before* it cost her the promotion.

I, too, felt badly that the organization had somewhat set her up—using and promoting her strengths and then turning on her when she overused them. But I also knew that in corporate America, when it comes right down to it, holding on to executive sponsorship is always tricky. By the time you reach the executive level, you are expected to behave in a situationally appropriate way, and you don't get many chances to screw up because what you do is so visible to the rest of the organization.

When it comes to Trap 2, the ego's response is to trust the rules, trust one's expertise, and turn to knowledge for guidance on how to lead. The playbook on emotional intelligence tells us to, instead, check in with other people about how they are thinking and feeling in a given situation—and to ask what they may need from us—so we can respond not as technical experts but as *leaders* who adjust to inspire, motivate, and foster each employee's potential to contribute and move the organization forward.

EQ Antidote: Recognizing, Reading, and Responding

Have you heard pieces in the stories of Gary or Tanya that resonate with your own interactions at work? Do you sometimes find yourself brandishing your technical skill as a factor to put your people back in their place or claim it as an excuse for not responding to feedback that you receive on your leadership performance? Do you hear regular commentary that you are a brilliant practitioner (lawyer, programmer, salesperson, etc.) while also catching grumblings or even formal feedback that you're a little weak on the people skills?

Or maybe, upon reflection, you realize that you sometimes fall back on your field expertise in situations where you might do better to work your leadership magic and watch your people soar as they put their own professional skills to work.

If you are beginning to discover traces of Ego Trap 2 at play in your own performance—believing that your technical skills trump your leadership skills—the three Rs of recognizing, reading, and responding can help to ground you in your role as an interpersonally savvy leader, not just the field expert to be admired or even feared.

I invite my clients who struggle with this particular trap to first look within—it's important that they consciously *recognize* how they are feeling in a given situation and notice any impulses to react from the gut as a technical expert (that's self-awareness). Does the executive have an instinct to spout knowledge to a team when they face a dilemma rather than patiently sit and listen as the team talks it through for a while? Does the executive have the urge to take notes (as Tanya did at the big meeting) or jump on someone's computer and start hacking away at the financial worksheet just because that is what the exec is really good at or is used to doing in a previous role? The goal is to tune in to those impulses so that the leader can control and moderate them, rather than being controlled by them. Many of the executives I work with who fall into this trap struggle mightily with perfectionism and all its unhealthy corollaries. Accepting that others can do a competent job will keep you focused on the important strategic work of an executive, instead of the nit-picking work of a subject matter expert.

Next, I encourage these executives to look outward—to *read* the cues from the people around them to get a better handle on what others may be feeling in a certain situation and what they may need (empathy alert!). Has the whole meeting room gone quiet because the team senses you don't trust their opinions? Do employees bring you unfinished work because they know you will make changes to it anyway, relying more and more heavily on your input (and feeding your self talk that your technical skills are needed: "I can't get less involved in the technical problem solving—clearly no one else is capable of doing the work independently.")

The final piece of the puzzle is to *respond* appropriately. The goal here is to take the internal and external information that the executive has gathered and use it to calibrate an emotionally intelligent response, rather than an ego-based one (self-control). Instead of jumping in with recommendations to solve a problem, the leader may ask the group to work through the answer. If the group comes up with a recommendation that started with the leader's idea, the leader might let the group take credit for it. With this approach, the leader's need to be the smartest person in the room (ego) is set aside in favor of building the team's technical skills and overall confidence (EQ).

As for our EQ-challenged executive, Gary, my coaching notes reveal that the three big EQ tools—self-awareness, empathy, and self-control—could provide Gary with a path forward, one that would allow him to retain his employment as CLO and raise his leadership game to match his legal game. My EQ prescription for Gary called for him to continue his development by:

- Focusing on the triggers that brought out his tendency to solve people challenges with technical solutions (self-awareness)
- Remembering that his way is not the only way and seeing that "failure" can provide employees with some of the richest learning opportunities (empathy)
- Giving people time to think for themselves and come to their own conclusions without giving them the "right" answer immediately (self-control)

After realizing that his job was in jeopardy, Gary finally made some changes. It wasn't easy, but he began to let go of his need to always be in control of interactions and instead worked on being present in conversations so he could notice and acknowledge the emotional undercurrents of his interactions. He stopped taking calls in the middle of conversations, and he encouraged employees to come into his office with questions, no longer dismissing them with a wave.

I spoke with Gary's boss at the conclusion of our engagement together and he said, "I have to say that Gary seems to be a different person, and everyone is commenting about it. So far, there appears to be real change occurring. Honestly Jen, I don't recall seeing so radical a change in behavior in any employee I've ever had." I, too, was impressed with the attitude change I had seen in Gary, and hoped that he would be able to maintain these initial EQ improvements over the long term. Only time would tell (see Ego Trap 8 for more!). Although Gary had worked hard on his interpersonal behavior, the real game changer came simply from shining the light on his blind spots, not from some dramatic shift in his core character. In most cases, the lower a person's self-awareness—and Gary's was low—the higher the coaching potential.

In a Nutshell

As a leader, you likely recognize the value—and *necessity*—of your employees and team members when it comes to creating business success. You know you can't do it alone, and many of your executive colleagues would agree with you. In a conversation with 1,700 CEOs and senior public sector leaders, the IBM Institute for Business Value found that 71 percent of these leaders view human capital as essential to "driving outperformance." In fact, it was the number-one factor cited, ahead of customer relationships and innovation of products and services.

If you are a leader with a tendency to fall into Ego Trap 2, the challenge may be in following through on this belief that your team is what matters most. It can only happen if you make a concerted effort to shift your values: you must transform from one who possesses and leverages the technical know how to one who trusts his team's competence and relies on his people to make the organization a success. Your own success depends on it. By letting go of your need to be the expert, stepping out of your own comfort zone, and investing energy in developing your team's expertise, you will be able to shift from a technical expert who has a leadership title to a people-savvy leader who uses her expertise as a platform to help others succeed.

APPLYING THE THREE R'S

Recognize the moods and impulses within yourself (self-awareness) that may tempt you to react as a technical expert; learn to identify the situations in which your leadership matters more than your expertise.

Read how these moods and impulses affect others who work for you and their ability to deliver results. Identify what the group really needs from you to succeed so you are primed to respond as a supportive leader rather than a hard-driving expert (empathy).

Respond with patience and understanding, knowing that people will not always be able to track technical issues as quickly as you are, and be willing to answer questions with respect and genuine interest. Don't be the first to jump in with an answer, and avoid involving yourself in technical problems; if you've delegated a task, let your team work through the issue (self-control).

Ego Trap 3

Surrounding Yourself with More of You

Jeanine, a successful business owner of three shoe stores in a tri-city area, inadvertently fell into Ego Trap 3: *surrounding yourself with more of you*. After a longtime general manager retired from one of the stores, Jeanine—a sparky, middle-aged entrepreneur with a gift for sales—took replacing the person very seriously. The role of general manager was vital to the success of her company: it involved managing part-time employees and their weekly schedules; coordinating directly with Jeanine on inventory and accounting; ensuring high-quality customer service; and managing many other tasks that kept the stores running smoothly on a daily basis. This was a make-or-break decision for Jeanine.

She whittled the list of applicants down to three qualified candidates. Madeline, the first to arrive for an in-person interview, reminded Jeanine of a younger version of herself: spunky and hungry to learn the business, with many years of sales experience (as indicated on her résumé and as discussed during the interview). The two women had a few interests in common, too, and discovered they knew a number of the same people around town. Jeanine, sensing kismet and going with her gut, hired Madeline on the spot without checking references or waiting to interview the next two people. Jeanine reached out to me six months later when she noticed the first signs of trouble. Madeline was indeed a great salesperson, just like Jeanine. Unfortunately, like Jeanine, she preferred the sales floor to administrative tasks. Madeline lacked the organizational skills required to handle the accounting books and she didn't manage personnel effectively, ultimately costing the business roughly 10 percent in revenue because of poor inventory management and an increase in employee turnover. Jeanine had fallen into Ego Trap 3—surrounding herself with people like herself—and one of her stores was paying the price for this naïve yet common leadership slip. If Jeanine didn't replace Madeline soon, it wouldn't be long before her regular customers stopped coming back because the store didn't carry what they needed. In addition, employee turnover costs were mounting and threatened to eat up all her profit. Jeanine was faced with a tough decision, a dilemma that could have been avoided if she had spent more time determining whom to bring onboard and why.

Jeanine was not alone in her hiring mistake. When it comes to building an executive team, nearly every CEO or business owner will say to me: "I'm a really good judge of character, so I go with my gut." Too often, as a result, these leaders dispense with a thorough interview, and that perfect person turns out to be a terrible technical or cultural fit, resulting in more turnover or, worse, an employee who stays and makes everyone else miserable. Other leaders, trusting their own instincts, hire or promote members of their team based on rapport, eschewing evidence-based hiring processes and best practices to follow their "gut feeling." You might ask yourself, "Well, if I *am* a great judge of character, why is that bad? After all, I've been successful." This thinking may sound logical, but it's actually riddled with blind spots.

The risk is that you may end up surrounding yourself with people you probably "click with" because they share your same strengths, values, and ways of thinking—exactly the people least likely to challenge your decisions or catch the balls you drop. That's a risky game to play in a competitive marketplace, where diversity of thought and creative offerings are what keep organizations alive. When you surround yourself with more of "you," you set up—or, worse, institutionalize—blind spots that can prevent you from seeing oncoming challenges.

When you hire others who live on your wavelength, you unintentionally create a support system of people who are not equipped to challenge you, to question your thinking, or to offer you a different perspective and direction. You essentially become trapped in a self-made bubble, missing opportunities to hear valid dissent, better approaches, or alternative ideas. Stagnation, disengagement, monotony, and rigidity: these are all organizational symptoms when the leader suffers from Ego Trap 3. Putting your emotional intelligence to work during the hiring and promoting process can help prevent these blind spots from occurring and give you a new way to think about what makes for the "perfect" hire.

A Closer Look at the Trap

By the time individuals reach the level of executive or thriving business owner, they understand the value of putting together the right team. For the new CEO, painstaking efforts often go into deciding which team members stay, which may have to go, and what kind of new team members to bring onboard. The owner of a growing business realizes she can no longer be the person to stuff boxes in the back room, make trips to the post office, and stand on the showroom floor; staffing is about finding team members who can do these jobs in a way that reflects the company's values and brand promise, as well as add value beyond job scope to improve the organization. The question for many CEOs and business owners is, "Now that you can no longer do it all alone, what kind of team will you hire, build, and cultivate to support you?"

The value of effective teams in the workplace has long been highlighted in business articles, in college courses, and by organizational development specialists inspired by management guru Peter Drucker, who began writing about teams in the early 1990s, and Jon Katzenbach and Douglas

Smith, who first published *The Wisdom of Teams* in 1993.[1,2] Over the past three decades, organizations across the globe have invested millions of dollars in workplace team-building initiatives as well as off-site trust-building retreats like ropes courses and mock survival games. The goal in these endeavors is often to ensure that individual team members "gel," play nicely, and work together effectively. These are all important attributes of a team. What if, however, organizations and leaders also need to pause and consider the opposite issue? What if leaders' preferences and points of view so closely match those around them that they develop collective blind spots? This represents a significant organizational risk that can escape the collective consciousness until it's too late.

Ironically, I have found in my work with CEOs that when the executive team gets along too splendidly—when they all agree on the same approach in a matter of minutes, when they are in the same mental groove, and when meetings draw short because there's no disagreement or challenge taking place among the members—it may be a red flag that points to an unbalanced team or one that is operating on mediocrity. The team may be happy and getting along well in these cases, but they may also have fallen into Ego Trap 3—when the leader has managed to become surrounded with miniature versions of himself, rendering the organization's most valuable asset, human capital, into business-as-usual drones. When this happens, the result can be a lack of challengers in the group—no different thinkers to say, "Hey, have you considered this possibility?" or "What happens if the bottom falls out on that approach?" We call these people "provocateurs," and they play a vital role in creating innovation and challenging the status quo. Just remember, when the executive team has too many look-alike members, the organization risks becoming vulnerable and stagnant.

Ego Trap 3 occurs when you hire, promote, or cultivate a strategic team that is made up of people who are similar to you in key ways, such as background, race, gender, age, strengths, values, or mind-set. For Jeanine, the business owner mentioned earlier, the fall into Ego Trap

3 involved hiring someone who had her same sales strengths, shared some of her interests in running and travel, and knew some of the same people around town. For other leaders, the magnetic attraction to a candidate might involve having a degree from the same school, being around the same age, or having a similar personality type.

It's perfectly natural to be drawn to someone who understands you. You may finish each other's sentences and bristle at the same annoyances. You think, "Wouldn't it be great to work with *that person?*" Regardless of the type of similarities, Ego Trap 3 comes into play when the leader gives priority to hiring or promoting a person who is similar to her, rather than consciously seeking out individuals who are able to bring a unique approach or mind-set to the team or to offer the special skill set necessary for success. Ego Trap 3 may actually be more sinister than the others, because it lures you with a mirror that reflects your strengths, your style, and your language, while silently multiplying your (admittedly few and relatively minor) shortcomings. I know, a "mini me" is as much fun to be around as *you* are. But wouldn't it be even better to surround yourself with people whose skills are complementary but not identical to yours? With people who would thrive in areas you would rather hand off anyway?

When Your Team Looks Like You

Ego Trap 3, surrounding yourself with more of you, forms a sort of opposite to Ego Trap 1, ignoring feedback that you don't like. Whereas with Trap 1 leaders tend to create a culture in which *people are afraid to tell the honest truth* when they disagree, with Trap 3, the leader has handpicked a group of like-minded *individuals who sincerely and honestly don't disagree,* even when perhaps they should. When a meeting is held and no one dissents, it's not due to fear of repercussions, as it would be with Trap 1. It's because the group thinks alike and maybe even defers naturally to the leader's perspective. This can lead to trouble, as it did with a national independent oil company that hired me to help profile and train more than five hundred employees on communication style.

By the time I conducted a meeting with the executives of this organization, my team had gathered information pointing to signs of hiring bias within the organization. It was a matter of communication styles: 360-degree assessments showed that almost everyone on the executive team had a *direct communication* style, which meant these executives tended to be faster paced, risk tolerant, arbitrary, and action oriented. While most groups' natural communication style shakes out to be about a fifty-fifty split between those who prefer direct versus indirect communication, the young CEO, John, an affable guy reminiscent of JFK Jr., had managed to surround himself with individuals who were *just like him*. Ego Trap 3 had sprung.

Making matters more complicated, hiring bias had also occurred at the lower levels of the organization—but in the opposite direction. By the time all of the 360-degree reports came in, the ratio across the company outside of the executive team indicated that 70 percent of individuals preferred *indirect communication*—slower paced, risk averse, methodical, thoughtful, and process oriented. It was time for me to share the stunning results with the executive team.

We met in the boardroom at the company's Houston headquarters. There were nine senior executives (all male) who reported to John, who was very charismatic and charming, usually winning people over to his side with ease, even if he was known for his strong opinions and stubborn nature.

I began by sharing the feedback data from the company, explaining the 70 percent to 30 percent figure, and asked some questions to stimulate the executives' thinking on why the scale was tipped so far to one side. They started to voice concerns, similar to mine, that hiring bias could be occurring. Then we got to the executives' own reports, which offered the following results: nine out of ten in the room were direct communicators, making the imbalance 10 percent to 90 percent in the opposite direction of the rest of the organization. The room exploded with comments: "No wonder it feels like we're stuck in the mud!"; "Our expectations around senior managers making quick decisions isn't reasonable"; "We are on complete opposite ends of the spectrum."

Finally, John spoke up and called the situation out for what it was—a severe imbalance in communication styles, leading to a deficit in one approach among executives and another among the "troops." Not only was there a stark polarity in communication styles at the company, but the executives were essentially pitted against the rest of the organization. As John put it, the executives had all been frustrated by what he described as the "gas and the brakes." The slower it seemed the organization moved on strategic initiatives, the harder the executives pushed on the gas. They were a team of like-minded peers reinforcing one another's desire to pick up the pace: "Yes, we *are* moving too slow. Let's up the consequences for missing expectations."

At the same time, the rest of the organization, bolstered by its opposite like-minded majority, pushed down on the brakes in equal measure and reinforced the need to do the same with each other. "Mahogany row (*unflattering slang used to refer to senior management coined by those in operations*) doesn't understand what's involved in this decision. We cannot rush into this without really analyzing all the data. The consequences to us are nothing compared to what a mistake will cost this company." Thus, what ensued was a continual stop–start dynamic that not only frustrated all the employees, but also stymied the company's ability to grow and thrive.

Sadly, the epiphany that day came too late. Despite the momentum in overall effectiveness, within eighteen months of my meeting with the senior executives, the company was bought out by a firm headquartered out of state, leading to the loss of hundreds of jobs. This example shows just how vital it is for senior executives, and those responsible for helping them hire, to be on the lookout for hiring bias that could tip the company in one direction for long enough that the damage becomes irreparable.

How can an organization like this oil company get so far off track and out of touch? This disconnect is often the telltale sign that hiring mistakes and random team-member selection have been silent predators, eating away at the company's future. Even the best intentions to find the right candidate for a position can easily become derailed by hiring bias. It's not an exaggeration to say that interviewers may gravitate toward a candidate because he plays the same sport as the interviewer or because they look alike. I know of one person who believes he was hired for an entry-level job early in his career because he and the hiring manager agreed on where to find the best pizza in Brooklyn.

Research from the *American Sociological Review* appears to confirm that this superficial hiring bias is real. The reasoning? According to *CNN Money,* which reported on the findings from the *American Sociological Review,* "Employers value feelings of comfort, validation, or excitement when meeting with job candidates over a prospect's superior cognitive or technical skills." Case in point: the *ASR* study found that certain individuals doing the interviewing made exceptions to hiring guidelines to help move forward an interviewee who had a similar background to that of the interviewer. As *CNN Money* noted, interviewers "would consciously lower the technical bar for candidates with whom they had a great spark."[3] Something seems to happen in the brain at an unconscious level that makes it easy to fall into Ego Trap 3.

The social psychology research also tells us that it's natural for people to group like objects together and to develop "cognitive biases" as a result.[4] A *Harvard Business Review* article entitled "Hiring Without Firing" reminds us, too, of the well-researched "halo effect" (also mentioned in the Ego Trap 1 chapter), the human tendency to allow one positive characteristic to outshine all others, such as charisma or pedigree.[5] That same article notes that the most widespread bias of all is the predisposition to highly rate individuals who are like ourselves. The reason? Doing so not only reinforces our own self-worth but boosts our sense of security that we "know what we are buying" over the risky sense of less familiar options.

Fortunately, the research also shows us that this bias can be overcome. For example, when simply encouraged to form more accurate impressions, people become more able to see others as individuals and avoid "automatic reliance on stereotypes" that might otherwise influence a job candidate's chances.[6] Just as useful, a person's motivation to avoid stereotypical thinking can also make a difference. Avoiding Ego Trap 3 may start, quite simply, with your own recognition of this pitfall and your wish to prevent it.

The Diversity Deficit on High

So if leaders fall prey to hiring only those who look like themselves, what happens to the much-touted ideal of a diverse workplace? The value of diversity, like effective team-building, has been a common topic of discussion within the workplace over the past decade. Unfortunately, although diversity initiatives are now commonplace at many organizations—especially larger ones—diversity is still often sorely lacking at the executive level. For example, according to a report by *Diversity Inc.* magazine in 2011, of all Fortune 500 CEOs, only 1.2 percent (six) of them at the time were black, only 1.8 percent (nine) were Asian, and only 1.2 percent were Hispanic.[7] The rest, a whopping 479 CEOs, were Caucasian. As for women, only nineteen (or 4 percent) of Fortune 500 CEOs at the time were female. Clearly, at the highest level of organizations, we still have a lack of representation in terms of gender and race.

If we look at executive teams as a whole, rather than just the CEO position, diversity likewise tends to be scarce. I see this every day when working with well-meaning executive teams in the corporate world. For example, not long ago I was sitting with one of my clients, a CEO, on our first meeting together when he shared with me an organization chart with photos of his executive committee. Looking back at me from the chart were the faces of eight white males between the ages of forty and sixty. I gently but directly asked this CEO, "So, if I'm a female candidate, why would I want to work for you?" My question caught him off guard. He studied the pictures more closely. "Oh, my gosh," he said with sincerity. "I didn't even notice that." Admittedly, he worked in a typically male-dominated industry, but in my view, the lack of women or ethnic minorities on my client's executive committee wasn't just a matter of political incorrectness or unappealing aesthetics to a female candidate. I would argue that his team was vulnerable, because of the homogeneity of the team, to missing something important when surveying the business landscape and developing strategy.

Interestingly, a 2012 study by Thomson Reuters of major global and European indexes revealed that organizations with 30 percent or more women managers and board members "outperformed" those with less than 20 percent women. This was particularly evident during quarters two through four, when financial markets were noticeably volatile.[8] A 2012 report by Credit Suisse Research Institute noted similar findings. After analyzing more than two thousand global companies, the institute found that companies with one or more female board members had produced "higher average returns on equity, lower gearing, better average growth, and higher price/book value multiples" than those with no female board members.[9]

Although the proportion of women on boards appears to be on the rise, lack of diversity at the top is not an imagined issue.[10] One recent survey showed the following:

- Hispanics represent only 3.28 percent of board members and 2.90 percent on executive teams, about one-fifth of the 15 percent they represent in the U.S. population.
- African Americans represent 8.77 percent of board members and 4.23 percent of executive teams, compared to being 13 percent of the U.S. population.

- Women represent 18.04 percent of board members and 19.87 percent of executive teams, or less than one-half their proportion of the national population.[11]

It's easy for a lack of diversity to happen at the highest levels, sometimes due to bias and sometimes because of a legitimate talent shortage. My goal for this chapter is not to debate the reasons for this lack of diversity or to get into a political discussion, but instead to highlight that a lack of diversity in the highest echelons of the company can have a significant and negative business impact.

I hope that, by hearing these startling figures, you will be spurred to look at your own organization to consider how far it may have to go in eradicating any hiring biases. You will have a chance to develop the awareness needed to catch this subtle dynamic, take steps to prevent it, and craft your own multifaceted and exceptional team. My next hope is to provide you with tools that can help you foster diversity of all kinds on the executive team, not just in terms of race, age, and gender, but also in terms of strengths, personality types, communication styles, and personal and professional backgrounds. Without this diversity of approach and ideas, you risk giving your team blinders that could lead to reduced innovation, lapses in judgment or quality, and financial losses like those seen by Jeanine, the small business owner, or on a much grander scale by investment banks like JP Morgan Chase á la the $6 billion "London Whale" losses in the spring of 2012 (stay tuned for more).

YOU KNOW YOU'VE FALLEN INTO EGO TRAP 3 IF...

- You don't have anyone in your inner circle who has a work or communication style opposite your own.
- Decisions among the executive team are made quickly and easily with minimal challenging viewpoints. (Although, you gotta love those short meetings!)

- Your executive leadership team lacks diversity (e.g., all are white males in their 50's).
- Challengers in the company are often ostracized, labeled as nay-sayers, or seen as "just not team players."
- Your company lacks a formal, structured interviewing and selection process, and managers, including you, have the latitude to hire on "gut feel" with little or no evidence of competency or indication that the person's skills match the job's requirements.

The Battle of Ego vs. EQ

It is always unfortunate to see an otherwise successful, conscientious executive miss one or two signals that their ego is starting to overpower their EQ. It often sneaks up on them and leaves them with the long clean-up work that is then required.

King Jamie

For a case study lesson on ego and EQ, let's look at the $6 billion trading losses suffered by JP Morgan Chase in 2012 and the company's well-respected CEO, Jamie Dimon. There is much debate over how Mr. Dimon could have let this incident happen on his watch, given his reputation for keeping an eagle eye on all corners of the organization.

We likely won't be able to answer that question here, as the details of the incident continue to unfold. And yet the story demonstrates a sort of tug-of-war between ego and EQ that helps us see how this trap—or any of the traps for that matter—may not always represent a simple issue.

Dimon is described by colleagues as having a high EQ and a high sense of "humanity." He also seems to possess empathy, displayed in his regular practice of asking team members who have been tasked with making a big hire: "Would you want your child to work for that person?" He appears to also understand the importance of having people challenge him, a prudent safeguard against Ego Trap 3. When asked about "the Cult of Jamie," Dimon has responded, "If people talk about the 'Cult of Jamie' because they respect me and listen to me and trust me—then that's not a bad thing," he says. "But if you mean the 'Cult of Jamie' because I'm the boss and no one can question me, that's not a good thing." Empathetic yet shrewd, Dimon has been known to fire executives when he felt they were no longer right for the job.[12]

And yet when we go searching for answers on how so many risky trades at the London office escaped Dimon's eye—Dimon was typically well versed in company activities at all levels—many of us find ourselves looking to the executive at the helm during it all. Could it be that Dimon took his eye off the ball and did not have a single executive on his team able to raise red flags for him? As *Vanity Fair* journalists William Cohan and Bethany McLean put it: "Basic risk-management practices were skipped, warning signs were ignored, and denial ran rampant through the executive suite. Dimon violated his own rule, which is 'Trust, but verify.'"[13] We may never know the exact reason why such sloppy practices got past Dimon, but I have to wonder whether there was some degree of like-mindedness among his executive team that made it easy for them to overlook red flags. Perhaps their single-minded trust in Dimon and his watchfulness created a type of tunnel vision that left people on autopilot. And let's not forget the dynamic that essentially made Dimon his own boss: he was chairman of the board as well as CEO.

Dimon himself explains that he got "complacent." And who could blame him after his bank emerged from the economic crisis of 2008 unscathed? When asked about his initial casual dismissal of the trading losses, he explained his response by noting that his direct reports had "told him everything was fine. 'I was assured by them,' he says, 'and I have the right to rely on them.'"[14] Of course he does. But was Dimon missing a challenger or provocateur in his group? CEOs do, to some degree, have to rely on their executive teams to be their eyes and ears. This is the reason it is so important to have people on your team who see and hear things differently than you do. Instead of seeing them as contrarians or annoyances, encourage them to question and challenge, and safely allow them to bring their own unique perspectives to the table.

Although some have cast Dimon as egotistical, with one colleague calling him "narcissistic" and another referring to him as "King Jamie," another shares that, while Dimon has a healthy-sized ego, he can also laugh at himself.[15] I see Dimon not as an egregious egomaniac, but as representative of many CEOs who are excellent at what they do and bear the confidence of that reality, but who nonetheless are just as human as the rest of us. Confidence can turn into complacency; they sometimes make mistakes. The point for the rest of us? Even if Ego Trap 3 is not your Achilles heel, it (and any of the other ego traps in this book) can still creep up and bite you if you are not paying attention. This is a reality that executive leaders have to contend with. They must take steps to challenge themselves, raise their awareness, and rigorously pursue growth in themselves and others. These are traits emotionally intelligent leaders have in common. Keeping your EQ sharp will help you avoid the slippery slope of egotism and complacency, and will help put some useful protections in place that King Jamie likely covets in hindsight.

Going Beyond Gut Instinct

Clearly, there is an element of ego that can be dangerous and that sets leaders up for the fall into Ego Trap 3. The thinking goes something like this: "I'm good at what I do, therefore I represent the model for the ideal job candidate." The temptation is to take this self-valuing and turn it into an *overvaluing*, in which the leader assumes, often unconsciously, that the goal is to hire little versions of herself to run the different areas of the organization.

Not all leaders who fall into Ego Trap 3 are this extreme. Many do value different perspectives, approaches, and strengths—in theory. The question is: What happens *in practice*? When it comes time to do the actual hiring or promoting, some leaders may still struggle to overcome the natural bias to hire or promote those like themselves. These leaders may naturally seek what feels comfortable or familiar, defaulting to a point of view of "What feels good to *me*?" and "What is normal in *my world*?"

It can just be easier to hire those like you. It's comfortable to work with people who communicate like you, who have a similar educational background, or who think like you do. You can trust them to do what you would in your absence, and they are easier to get along with. It's also pleasant to work with individuals who don't question your perspective, who never make you feel defensive, and who consistently respect your ideas. It's not a matter of being selfish; it's just that the ego naturally seeks harmony and peace. Surrounding yourself with people who think like you do can be a lot more comfortable than interacting with those who see the world as white when you see it as black, who occasionally call your strategies into question, or who offer up ideas and strategies that sound, to you, off the wall.

Yet, stepping back, it's probably fair to say that you didn't get where you are today as an executive or business founder by staying comfortable. Over the years, you surely have put the organization first, whether by working long hours, skipping paychecks, or dealing with difficult customer or employee issues. By being willing to step out of your comfort zone and push beyond your own ego needs when it comes to hiring and promoting, you once again put the organization first. That's EQ at work.

On the flip side of ego is EQ. Leaders with high EQ have a healthy sense of self, but not an overinflated one, which helps them stay open to the strengths, unique viewpoints, and special skill sets that others will bring to the table. What's more, leaders with high EQ are willing to do some (okay, maybe lots of) adjusting. Instead of immediately hiring candidates who feel right on a gut level ("I could really work with him" or "I just have a good feeling about her"), leaders with strong EQ know to check in with themselves and see if any biases are playing out.

These leaders have also identified accountability partners who can help them check for blind spots. They then have the self-discipline to let the candidate-selection process play out in full, so that all individuals are considered, rather than take shortcuts through the process as soon as they find someone they click with.

Finally, those with high EQ understand that their own needs must not supersede the needs of others in the organization. With this degree of empathy and self-awareness, these leaders increase their success in bringing individuals on board who spark new thinking and help foster a culture in which questioning is okay. When these challenges and questions come, leaders with high EQ don't take it personally but instead view them as signs of healthy conflict and heightened opportunities for success.

So what is the good news about the sometimes challenging shift from ego to EQ while building your organizational or executive team? You can find people who are both easy to work with *and* who are willing to bring a fresh perspective to the table. Hires with high EQ who have been selected based on specific job fit and culture criteria will not only produce greater performance results, they will also feel comfortable being honest. And they will be able to adapt to working with all sorts of personalities (including yours!). By building a diverse, emotionally intelligent leadership team, you mitigate risk and open up opportunity for fresh ideas and innovation.

EQ Antidote: Recognizing, Reading, and Responding

So, how do you effectively build a diverse team, one with different backgrounds and approaches, rather than a team composed of look-alikes in terms of age, gender, communication style, strengths, personality, and background? How do you gather individuals around you who can also serve as questioners, challengers, and provocateurs?

With EQ at play, you will remember to check in with yourself during the hiring and promoting process to identify any biases you may have toward candidates who are like you. Even without immediate chemistry with a candidate, you will be able to ask, "What does the other person offer that complements and counterbalances my strengths and weaknesses?" This is all about *recognizing* what's going on inside of you (self-awareness) and being ready to tweak your approach when needed to avoid bias and to increase your openness to candidates who bring a unique perspective and skill set to the team.

Next, with EQ leading the way, you will be able to step outside your own approach and consider the value of others' approaches (empathy). With this open-minded attitude, you gain an ability to *read* or appreciate strengths different from your own that candidates may bring to the role. With empathy, "other" individuals become less foreign and you grow capable of bringing them onto your team even if they are different from you.

Finally, it's time to *respond*. The candidates have been considered; who are you going to hire or promote? This is where self-control can come into play, helping you carefully consider your candidates and match them to the *organization's needs*, in addition to your own. It's not about hiring loyalists or "mini me's." It's about gathering individuals who have the expertise needed to lead their area of the company with success. Following your organization's standard hiring practices, rather than short-cutting through the interview process, can also help you stay on track. It never helps when you send the "Do as I say, not as I do" message that comes with skirting your own rules.

As you begin to build a team with varied backgrounds, styles, strengths, and personalities—and encourage a culture of debate and conversation—there may be moments of newness, discomfort, and challenge. Use your EQ to remain open to and nonjudgmental of these challenges. And don't forget about making sure those you hire have EQ too. Why? If you are hiring challengers just to have challengers on the team, you are sure to be miserable if these individuals don't have EQ. Instead, aim to find people who think differently than you do and who also have enough EQ to be honest with you, while balancing that with the self-control necessary to get along with others.

WHAT TO DO WHEN YOU'RE SURROUNDED BY YOU

Uh-oh! You've awakened to the realization that everyone on your team looks or thinks an awful lot like you do. What next? If you discover that your team is homogeneous or you find signs of a culture in which it's important to maintain the status quo, it's time to shift toward encouraging diverse opinions and thinking. Here are some tips to help you do this.

1. *Request opposing points of view.* You can start by assigning devil's and angel's advocates in executive meetings to ensure that all sides of an issue have been considered.
2. *Find the questioner in your life.* Go to the person in your life who never hesitates to tell you exactly what he thinks and whose opinion you respect (e.g., a sibling, coworker, your old college roommate). Use this person as a sounding board or pick her brain for new ideas on old topics. Instead of distancing yourself, regularly seek out this thought partner for insight and perspective.
3. *Join a CEO club.* There is a growing trend of leaders joining peer groups (like the Young Presidents Organization, Vistage, the CEO Roundtables, and Mastermind) because it provides a much-needed forum for exchanging ideas with peers who understand what you do at your level of responsibility. Consider joining one of these groups, where there is no fear of speaking honestly, and you can be sure you'll be challenged and inspired. Members of these organizations discourage tacit acceptance of what may be unsubstantiated ideas or anything that smells of being sold the proverbial "bill of goods."

These practices will help put some measures in place to hedge against the blind spots of Ego Trap 3. But remember: there is no replacement for a diverse and varied team.

Over time, if it becomes clear that new hires need to be brought onboard, it's important to find the wherewithal to make the change. This can be particularly hard for business founders who have had the same team by their side since the company's inception. Interestingly, what I have consistently seen in my work is that around the $100 million revenue mark, the start-up team hits a wall or a plateau. Since what got you there is rarely enough to keep you growing, it is only by bringing in new players that the organization can break through to the next level of success. Ultimately, the ability to build a strong team is in your hands. Are you ready to act?

In a Nutshell

Although it can be tempting to keep people around you who think like you do and who have the same instincts, this approach can lead to a team with the same strengths and little that offsets the same weaknesses. When you're hiring and promoting, are you looking for people who will challenge you and who think differently? Does your inner circle of advisors think differently, and is it okay for them to raise a contrary point of view?

As you can see, Ego Trap 1—ignoring feedback you don't like—and Ego Trap 3 go hand in hand. Not only do you need people on your team who have different perspectives than you (Trap 3), you also need to make sure that opposing viewpoints are allowed and encouraged at the highest levels (Trap 1). In essence, the goal here is to ensure that people are committed to organizational objectives and not just to "pleasing the boss." By building a diverse executive team, encouraging a culture where feedback and challenge are the norm, and putting a priority on avoiding hiring bias at all levels of the company, you can strengthen your own organization through a well-rounded roster and the natural checks and balances inherent in a diverse group.

APPLYING THE THREE R'S

Recognize that *your* qualities are not the only ones that are valuable to the business (self-awareness). Where are your weaknesses? How can hiring to your weaknesses help you build a well-rounded team?

Read the behaviors of others while temporarily setting aside your feelings and opinions. Just because others don't react exactly as you might shouldn't disqualify their contributions. In order to understand others you must learn to think as they do, not as you do (empathy).

Respond by challenging your initial good or bad reactions to a candidate. Force yourself to stick with an interview and gather well-rounded data about the person, even when you don't "click" right away (self-control). Sometimes the person who doesn't sync up with you in an interview turns out to have the very thing you need most.

Ego Trap 4

Not Letting Go of Control

Micromanager. It's a term we've all heard before, and not without at least a little disdain. As *Harvard Business Review* blogger Ron Ashkenas reminds us, many people complain about micromanagers, but none of us ever actually admit to being one.[1] Why would we? The micromanager is seen as meddling, untrusting, and counterproductive. The micromanager may even be thought of, ahem, as a *control freak*.

By the time individuals reach the level of CEO or senior executive, the era of micromanaging has long since passed. There's strategy to develop, markets to study, and decisions to make. There are talented people to develop, not to mention the constant daily needs of attending to the health and well-being of your business. There's simply no time or space for micromanaging once you reach the top echelons of the business.

Or is there?

In my years of working with and observing the senior executives and business founders in hundreds of companies, I have been surprised to see that micromanaging is not confined to the mid-level manager...it can show up all the way at the top, and may be most prevalent among young leaders who struggle with how to delegate and how much latitude to give their team. At the heart of micromanagement is an ego-based *failure to let go of control,* the subject of Ego Trap 4. A particularly dramatic example of this failure can be seen in the example of Craig, the CEO of a public accounting firm, who just couldn't keep his hands out of the organization's planning for a global leadership conference.

Craig, who was known for thinking that training was a waste of time and money, reluctantly agreed to offer a day of education after being pressured to do so—but only if the training could be added on to the end of an already scheduled global conference. Craig delegated the task of determining the content of the learning event to the chief administrative officer (CAO), who then delegated it to Charlene, the director of Human Resources, who was a strong professional with many years of experience in organizing and managing learning events.

Once Charlene started to dig into the planning, she expressed some concerns about adding a full day of training at the end of a weeklong conference. She worried that participants would be fatigued and that it would be difficult to meet the needs of a hundred global executives in such a short time frame. It was challenging enough to encapsulate executive leadership development that should take months into a single day, let alone adding it to the end of a busy conference. So Charlene suggested to her boss, the CAO, that the learning should be conducted separately from the meeting so it could be customized and better internalized. When Craig heard about Charlene's push back, he skipped past the CAO to Charlene directly and vehemently disagreed with her via e-mail. It would be too expensive, he argued, to have people travel again solely for training. In his words, "Since they are all there anyway, why can't we just do leadership training then?"

Realizing that there was no avoiding the single day of training, Charlene reached out to me and together we worked hard to create the best possible solution. Of course, I was clear up front regarding the disadvantages of this approach, and suggested that we set realistic expectations regarding the possible impact and outcomes. Our plan involved setting up breakout groups by functional area and delivering the most powerful content based on the venue constraints and audience profile. Charlene submitted her recommendations again, with associated costs, to her boss.

Again the CEO skipped the CAO, and responded directly to Charlene, stating, "Costs are too high. Agenda is attached. Have your folks on the skills training for hiring and policy administration/discipline adequate trainers to deal with 4 groups of 25." Huh? Charlene had trouble making sense of the CEO's directive, but she worried that if she replied with clarifying questions, she might come across as defensive or instigative.

When leaders like Craig insert themselves into the mix they can be cryptic and unclear in their commands, assuming others are on their wavelength and will easily see the thinking behind their instructions. Often this low-EQ, high-ego behavior simply complicates the situation for people who are just trying to do the best job possible. What's more, although Craig was dismissive of training on the one hand, on the other hand, he wanted to be involved in details he didn't know much about, like adult learning, learner needs assessments, best practices for content retention, and so on. This did not make for a good combination, and it put Charlene in a difficult predicament.

Charlene also found it confusing to have the CEO step in, as she now didn't know whether to advocate for what she felt would be most effective for the participants' actual learning or to put aside her own expertise in order to bow to the big boss's wishes and keep him happy. Add to that the fact that she reported to the CAO, not the CEO, and she was baffled about how to proceed. (Needless to say, the CAO was none too happy to be sidestepped either.) Charlene was suffering from the CEO's fall into Ego Trap 4: when the leader fails to let go of control over tasks that have been, or should be, delegated to other team members.

The case of Craig and Charlene points to a common theme I have seen over the past twenty years, especially when it comes to budget. Senior executives have a very hard time trusting that their high-level direct reports will be fiscally responsible. As a result, after delegating assignments, they meddle and micromanage. They fail to let go of control.

A look at Ego Trap 4 will remind you to examine whether you are focusing on the right *leadership* issues and tasks, or are getting caught up in less essential roles. Do you stay focused on developing strategy, growing and engaging talent, and keeping an eye on the overall business landscape? Do you stay informed of all of the significant goings-on at the company and making sure your team works well together? Or are you, like Craig, getting drawn into the way events are planned, how smaller amounts of money are spent, and the e-mail font everyone should use?

By shifting to an EQ-based approach, you will be able to clear your plate of any nitty-gritty activities that take you away from the more high-level responsibilities the organization needs you to fill. In the process you will strengthen your team as they gain opportunities to do the work they are good at without worrying about being second guessed or wasting their time.

A Closer Look at the Trap

Ego Trap 4 can confound both the traditional corporate CEO and the business founder who fails to let go of operational tasks as the business grows. Marty, a brilliant deal maker whose small business was bought by a Fortune 500 company, is one such example. A Latino gentleman with a fiery personality, Marty grew up in war-torn Colombia. His incredible street smarts and ability to negotiate his way out of difficult situations served him well as a business owner. He came to the United States as a teenager and by his late twenties was a thriving entrepreneur in a software development firm in Southern California. The small business did so well under his stewardship that it was sold to a Fortune 500 company, which allowed Marty and his team to continue operating as an independent subsidiary. As president of the subsidiary, Marty didn't see a need to change the way he led the company and went along with business as usual, including his mercurial tendencies. This meant that his good moods and bad moods were still clear to everyone.

Eventually, the parent company began to get more involved, giving Marty and his team more business, and eventually buying a similar company and putting Marty in charge of the merger of his former company and the newly acquired one. Diving deep into the details, Marty personally made all personnel decisions. Because he placed loyalty above all else, he very quickly eliminated many of the new company's employees without considering their talent or what the newly combined company would need going forward. He then set out to review the work of all employees, drafting his own versions of job descriptions and work flow. In his words, "I want to stay very focused and tactical regarding job roles over the next twelve months."

Marty also personally led all staff meetings. And because he had a hard time not being involved in the details, he had all functional areas report directly to him—which meant having *fourteen* direct reports. By the time I was brought in as a team advisor, Marty's group had grown to almost eighty employees and had been physically relocated to an office at the parent company's sprawling campus. Marty's visibility was growing, as were concerns about his ability to lead the company he was responsible for. Although his division was quite profitable, his group consistently missed deadlines and became known for team conflict. Making matters worse, these concerns were kept from Marty (see Trap 1), so he didn't realize that conversations about his future were happening at the CEO level. In fact, the parent company executives were so concerned about Marty's reaction to being told an executive coach was hired to help him, they asked me to call myself a "team advisor" to be less threatening.

After I met with Marty's fourteen direct reports, the following became clear:

- Marty often stepped into the middle of everything, which the team felt was making it difficult for the group to be "operationally optimized."
- Because Marty was in control of allocating all resources, personality issues between departments sometimes erupted as groups fought to protect their own turf and look good to Marty.

- Marty was rated lower as a leader than he otherwise might have been because he confused his team about who should do what. The group gave Marty an overall rating of six on a scale of one (low) to ten (high). Many said they would have given him an eight or a nine if he had been able to make expectations, roles, and responsibilities clearer.

All signs pointed to the reality that Marty was unable to relinquish control.

For a business founder like Marty, who had built the original company from bottom to top, stepping out of operations to play more of a conductor role just didn't come naturally. Not only did he feel he had valuable expertise to share by staying involved in operations, he enjoyed it! Getting involved in things like dictating how to beta test new software or deciding what piece of equipment to purchase came automatically to him, and he liked being a part of the action. It was a classic situation for a founder who had built the business from the ground up, and who had not yet figured out how to make the transition to leader of a larger organization.

The tendency for leaders like Marty to keep control comes primarily from the following sources:

1. A belief that nothing can get done with the same quality or standard without the leader's direct involvement
2. Failure to learn new executive leadership skills and behaviors
3. Concern about misconduct that could lead to a scandal
4. Fear of becoming irrelevant or out of touch
5. A misguided approach to demonstrating passion and desire to teach and educate others
6. Desire to be seen as a hardworking member of the team and not a fat-cat, ivory-tower executive

Let's look at a few of these in greater depth. The first of these reasons relates to "psychological inflation," what *Inc.* magazine describes as "a polite euphemism for egomania—the belief that you can perform a particular task better than anyone else."[2] In this case, leaders may have concerns about the competence of their team or may have a perfectionist streak and simply feel that no preventable error is acceptable. Naturally, if leaders feel they are better at executing certain responsibilities than the team members, it will be tempting to step in and do things for them.

Then there is the second reason, which relates to the old habits leaders may have of making operational decisions, habits that brought them much success in earlier days. If, when serving in the lower ranks of an organization or working as a start-up business owner, leaders were used to doing, operating, and executing, it will take conscious effort on their part to shift and grow into a new self-perception. This requires a changed paradigm about what they should be responsible for once they become executive leaders. Seeing responsibilities like building and motivating the executive team and setting the strategic direction of the company as a *primary* function of the leader's role may take quite a bit of mindful rewiring.

In addition, leaders may feel the need to stay heavily involved in operations in order to make sure the company avoids any major scandals. This is a fair goal. Business cases like Enron, Worldcom, and HealthSouth Corporation are enough to send shivers down the back of every senior executive about the dangers of losing touch with the goings-on inside their organization. This kind of fear is a common driver behind an executive's inability to let go of decision rights, especially those related to customers. This is understandable, though later in the chapter we will look at better ways of handling that fear than micromanaging.

YOU KNOW YOU'VE FALLEN INTO EGO TRAP 4 IF:

- You have more than ten direct reports.[3]
- You cannot help but get involved in seemingly minor details "just for peace of mind."

- You spend much of your time focused inward, on company operations, and very little looking outward at the industry or business landscape.
- When you are away from the office, decisions grind to a halt or it seems nothing gets done until you return, validating, of course, that you are indeed indispensable and your senior team is helpless without you.
- You see yourself as the ultimate quality-control inspector.
- You feel people need very detailed instructions in order to perform at their best.

The Battle of Ego vs. EQ

Ironically, in some cases micromanaging leaders may see themselves as low-ego, ultimate "servant leaders."[4] They may think: "Look at me, I am rolling up my sleeves and working side by side with the troops." In reality, what may look like helping isn't helpful at all, because the group often doesn't need another operator. They need a leader. In most cases, the leader's need to be involved slows down the work of the group, as other things sit and wait for the leader to review or approve them. This is the most common complaint I hear from employees who work for leaders caught in this trap.

Inc. magazine makes an interesting distinction between *control* and *leadership* that may help highlight how ego plays into Ego Trap 4:

Control is about making sure orders and work requirements are carried out by following management's plans and directions. Leadership, on the other hand, is based on setting clear objectives, delegating authority, relinquishing control, and trusting staff.[5]

When guided by control, the leader retains power so the ego remains appeased. When guided by the principles of leadership, the executive or business founder lets go of power, *empowering* the team instead and setting aside any ego needs to be directly involved. Only with the self-awareness, empathy, and self-control that come with EQ can leaders gain the understanding and discipline needed to cede control to the team so they can meet organizational objectives by exercising their own power and agency.

Sometimes, this trap plays out in a more well-meaning fashion, as it did for Marty, who simply had a passion for operations. While Marty wouldn't have strong-armed an employee as Craig did, he would certainly show up with a smile at one of his direct reports' desks, ready to make plans and settle on logistics for something that he should have had no part in.

Whether the leader refuses to give up control because of a strong personality, as with Craig, or because of a passion for operations, as with Marty, the ego guides the leader in Ego Trap 4 to make decisions and behave in ways that make him feel comfortable at the expense of others' comfort.

As for Marty, over time, upper management became more honest with him about their concerns, and eventually Marty realized with the help of coaching that he could not be so involved in everything. In fact, he recently hired a Chief Operating Officer (COO) to manage the team and run the operations, freeing him up to meet with customers and make deals. Marty's division is thriving today because he was able to take a hard look at his weaknesses, make some important decisions, and let his EQ exceed his ego.

When I recently checked in with Marty, asking him how he thought he would handle having a COO in place and the opportunity to step back, let go of some control, and stay focused on more strategic and directional issues, Marty admitted, "It will be so hard for me not to meddle because honestly I know this business better than anyone here." Making the transition would not be easy, but Marty took the first step by bringing the COO on board and committing to letting her do her job.

EQ Antidote: Recognizing, Reading, and Responding

If you should discover that staying out of operations and letting go of control is a challenge for you, begin by looking within. Ask yourself questions like:

- Is this something I should be this involved with?
- Have I delegated this to someone else but am I still too far in?
- Is my involvement slowing everything down?
- Am I just gathering information, or am I now in the middle of something, telling people what to do?
- What would happen if I took my hands off the wheel? What does that tell me about how well I have prepared my next-tier leaders for running the business?

Then, exercise your self-awareness and work to *recognize* when your ego is causing you to step too far into the weeds. You may feel that the visibility on the assignment is too high, you may realize that you distrust the teams' competence, or you may recognize an excitement or overzealousness to be involved yourself in a given project. Rather than let these emotions dictate how you proceed—by jumping into operations—step back and consider what the environment needs from you. That's where empathy and *reading* comes in.

"But, Jen," many clients will tell me, "I would *love* to delegate more and get out of the way, but I just can't. My team is already overworked." Or some clients will say, "My team is just not capable of this. They need more experience first." If you've thought these things, I want you to stop and *read* what's really going on. Did you wait until you knew everything before making decisions? Do all signs point to your team being capable and trustworthy, even if they may not approach things the same way you do? If so, what does your team need from you to be successful? Are you making efforts to connect them to the support they need, or have you created an environment in which your team knows you will do the task yourself, conditioning them to appear, and perhaps feel, incapable? If not, maybe it's time to fix the performance issues or replace them instead of working around them.

Just as important, what kind of messages are your team members sending you when you get involved? Do they thrive on your conversations or do they seem deflated? Do they seem energized or irritated and confused? If you were in their shoes, would you be comfortable with *your* boss being this involved, or would you find it too hands-on and demoralizing? These questions are meant to help you self-diagnose so you can tune in to what your team really needs from you to be successful, and so you too can find a new, deeper level of fulfillment in your role.

With a good *read* on your team and insight into your own ego state, you'll have the information you need to *respond* appropriately and consciously. If fear of overspending drives you, consider letting this worry go, trusting your team to be fiscally responsible. Is there past evidence of people going crazy on the company's dime, or is yours an irrational fear? If there is a budget already approved for the project, then remind yourself that as long as the project is on budget you should stay out of it. And if you feel uncertain of a team member's competence, take the leap of faith to let the person run with a smaller project on their own to cut their teeth and build your confidence in them. A major part of any leader's job is to develop a bench of capable talent. You'll only know how the person operates if you let her try. Lastly, don't be afraid of mistakes; they are sure to happen. They happened to you in the past and probably serve today as some of your best learning experiences. The same goes for your team.

In most cases, there is a certain sense of serenity that comes with surrendering and accepting that unintended consequences aren't always terrible. The worst that will happen is that some of your fears will come true, but you will have a new lens with which to view the situation. You will see the gaps, learning needs, job misfits, and assumptions that you failed to see from your controlling mind-set. These are invaluable tools you can now use to target where you want to improve the organization, focusing your passions and energy on goals that have much greater significance and impact.

In the end, you as a leader have to define for yourself when it is appropriate to get involved in a situation. It can be helpful to come up with some clear thresholds to guide you as to when to get involved in projects and decisions versus when you should stay out of the fray. For example, you might come up with a financial threshold, such as "I will be involved in any financial decision that involves more than X dollars, but anything below that my team is capable of handling." Or it may be that all safety issues must escalate to you. You can also find an accountability partner to call you on your controlling tendencies when you cross the line. By developing clearer guidelines for when to let go of control, inviting others to hold you accountable, and accepting that it may always feel uncomfortable to trust, you will develop strong tools to help you avoid the urge to micromanage.

WHAT TO DO WHEN YOU DON'T TRUST YOUR TEAM

You've taken a good look at the situation and realize that you don't trust your team to perform to your standards and expectations. Now what? For starters, I recommend that you do the psychological inflation test to see whether your own beliefs may be at the heart of the problem. Are you convinced that no one else can do the job as well as you? Do you think you alone can get the best result? If so, consider the possibility that your ego-based beliefs are causing you to micromanage rather than any real incompetence on the part of your team. Most management teams really do have the skills and potential to handle assignments well. The issue lies more with the leaders' inability to fully delegate and stay out of projects.

If you're stuck in Ego Trap 4, it's time to give your team members a try. You won't know whether they can perform unless you give them the opportunity. If, after you allow your team members to manage projects and handle tasks, some truly emerge as inept, you may have a performance issue on your hands that requires replacing a team member. But don't rush to judgment. It's important to give people time to grow and learn. Remember, mistakes are great learning tools. It's okay, too, for your people to use a different approach than you. After all, they're really *not* you; they never will be, and that's okay.

In a Nutshell

The question for some leaders may be how to give up control at a time when scandals are breaking every day. It's fine to delegate *in theory*, these leaders may say, but *in practice*, the CEO has to stay in the weeds because it's always the CEO who is responsible when the ship starts to sink. As one executive put it to me: "This can't fail. My fingerprints are all over it." And, if the CEO isn't mixed into operations, how will he catch a $6 billion mistake before it happens or prevent the 200-million-gallon oil spill?[6,7] It's a fair question. No leader wants a scandal to happen on her watch, be it a huge financial loss, a product that's harmed consumers, or an oil spill that damages precious wildlife.

Yet it is not by managing every decision or putting a personal seal on each and every company initiative that you as a leader avoid scandal and keep the company financially upright; instead, it is by *staying informed*. It's by having really good processes in place for keeping you aware of important company operations, metrics, issues, and challenges. It's by making sure that people feel comfortable being honest with you—allowing you to avoid Ego Trap 1—and that team members who have perspectives different from yours are capable of raising counter-perspectives and detecting red flags—allowing you to avoid Ego Trap 3. Although it may feel safer at first to stay *involved* in operations and execution, by instead focusing on staying *informed* of operations, you can better keep your head above the daily din and see more of what's going on across the organization. That, my friend, is the leader's job, not the daily grind.

It's not your job to stay in the details and micromanage every challenge the company faces in each and every department, but instead to lead your people in the strategic direction you envision. If you feel that you must micromanage, then you don't trust. And if you don't trust, you place artificial limits on your company's ability to grow.

APPLYING THE THREE R'S

Recognize that all roads lead to Rome, or at least many of them do. Is your way really the only way to proceed? Recognize that your "do it my way" impulse may not serve your organization well (self-awareness).

Read the situation and the employee to determine how much involvement you really should have (empathy). Is your leadership required in approving the purchase of every single iPhone for your legal team? No. Is it required in deciding on a capital expense of $1 billion? Probably.

Respond according to the results delivered and measure your reaction without overreacting either positively or negatively (self-control). If your employee managed the weekly meeting effectively—meaning that he made progress and fully engaged participants—congratulate your employee on a job well done, even if he didn't do it your way. Didn't get the results you desired? Respond with constructive and developmental input, not anger.

Ego Trap 5

Being Blind to Your Downstream Impact

The program for the company's annual leadership retreat was all set. The senior leadership team had worked for months to design an event that was sure to inspire the company's leaders, 80 percent of whom were female, who traveled in from three states to attend. But one morning, just ten days before the retreat, the CEO, Jim, burst into the office with a new idea. He had heard the story of a Navy SEAL on the radio on his way into the office that morning, and he thought that the SEAL would be just *perfect* for the keynote address. Full of energy and excitement, Jim asked his executive team to do whatever they could to get this guy.

Jim—whose self-deprecating humor and infectious laugh easily won people over—had his heart in the right place. But when the team listened to his request, all they really heard was, "To hell with what you all had planned. I want *what I want*—now." Everyone adjusted to the new idea, but Jim's impulsiveness would reverberate well beyond the closing ceremony of the company retreat. His circle of senior leaders, charged with the planning, told themselves, "Typical Jim. It doesn't seem to matter what we put together, he'll step in at the last minute with his own whims, regardless of how much planning we do."

How could positive energy like Jim's be a drag on the business? His intentions were good and it wasn't such a crazy idea to have a Navy SEAL appear as keynote speaker. But making a major change to the plan ten days before the actual retreat? What seemed like a "cool" idea to Jim quickly turned into a scramble for the senior operations leaders planning the event. And, as it turned out, the talk by the SEAL was received in a predictably lukewarm fashion by the predominately female audience.

Jim had unknowingly fallen into Ego Trap 5, being blind to his downstream impact. As a result, his well-meaning directive to bring in the Navy SEAL had the opposite consequence of his original good intention, demoralizing his team, dampening the planned retreat, and marring his credibility. To all of this, however, Jim was clueless.

Every decision you make as a leader ripples through your organization in waves, and the amplitude can become more intense the further "downstream" it flows. The power you wield at the top is by no means a bad thing—when your eyes are wide open to its total impact. Yet too many executives forget that the choices they make, even seemingly small ones, can have far-reaching effects throughout the organization.

Shifting priorities arbitrarily, feeling hot about a project one day and cold the next, making *everything* a priority at once so that nothing is prioritized—all of these behaviors, and others, can get in the way of sustaining the organization's long-term goals and cloud the company's vision. By clearly reading the potential effect your behaviors have on others—by *exercising empathy*—you can avoid the pitfalls of being blind to your downstream impact.

A Closer Look at the Trap

Ego Trap 5 is triggered when a leader engages in behavior, often impulsive or unplanned, that has a disruptive effect on the team or organization. The effect of this behavior is to often create significant challenges for those downstream, challenges that the leader may never even hear about. Yet the consequences will no doubt be felt in the lower employee morale and decreased motivation of those who feel that their time and strategic buy-in is not valued.

Scattering Papers and Sinking Boats

Ego Trap 5 often manifests itself as "executive attention deficit hyperactive disorder" (E-ADHD), in which the leader displays constantly changing priorities and an undependable strategic direction, or makes requests for urgent but menial tasks with immediate and unreasonable deadlines that stop all other work in its tracks. You can almost see the leader walking through the office tossing directives left and right, with a trail of dust and papers flying around in her wake as employees try to manage the resultant chaos. Not all leaders who demonstrate this behavior suffer from clinical ADHD, but the behavioral examples I have witnessed and have heard described to me mimic similar symptoms. And in fairness to you, business owners, there may be an actual biological condition at work. Research has shown that those diagnosed with ADHD are actually 300 percent more likely to start their own business.[1] For those of you who are not clinically ADHD, it is your frenetic energy that can send everyone around you into a tailspin. Although it may be difficult to completely extinguish the associated behaviors of attention deficit disorder or of a high-octane personality, as a leader it is critical that you manage the consequences of these tendencies for your larger organization.

Sometimes Ego Trap 5 plays out as a tendency to be a "submarine boss," a leader who is silent for a period of time, then suddenly surfaces and makes requests that create chaos and knock every other boat out of the water.

Other times it manifests as having an "initiative du jour," a pet project a leader directs his team to focus on one day, which is then switched to another project the following day. Another version of this occurs when a leader asks the group to change company strategy midstream, with little explanation or apparent logic. In interviews with team members, I often hear complaints that these changing directives from the boss seem to have more to do with whatever business book or article the leader is currently reading or the latest trend she sees reported in the *Harvard Business Review,* than they do with the well-thought-out, long-term plan that the executive team has already agreed to *as a team.*

This ungrounded approach, in addition to generating frustration among employees as their to-do lists mount, also tends to baffle the team, who often cannot understand how new initiatives fit into previous game plans. (Spoiler alert: they don't.) Team members just have to hope that the leader runs out of time to pick up the next business bestseller at the airport newsstand, lest they be obligated to start the next round of ungracious hoop-jumping to accommodate yet another new strategy. While the spirit of innovation engendered by leaders who sometimes fall into Ego Trap 5 is absolutely invaluable, this enthusiasm can become misplaced when leaders try to reflexively implement it without running through the normal checks and balances of the executive team, or better yet, one's own EQ filter.

QUESTIONS TO ASK BEFORE IMPLEMENTING YOUR IDEAS

Ego Trap 5 is sometimes triggered by the leader's bursts of creative energy. If your mind is a natural idea machine, you don't want to lose all the value that comes with fresh ideas and new approaches, and no one else does either. So keep the ideas coming! But as a safeguard against Ego Trap 5, make sure that any new ideas get considered from an emotionally intelligent perspective before implementing them to avoid disrupting the team's strategically focused and well-orchestrated efforts. Here are some questions that can help you consider all angles before proceeding.

1. How does the new idea fit with the organization's current strategic direction or day-to-day work flow?
2. Does this idea have the longevity and potential to justify a shift in focus?
3. How much time will it really take my team to execute this initiative?
4. What change in priority does this potential new initiative represent relative to what's already in the pipeline?
5. Are there any potential mixed messages I might be sending with this new direction or idea?
6. Have I invited my executive team to weigh in on the new initiative's value and whether it will advance or detract from the organization's established objectives?
7. Is this the right time to implement this idea?
8. Will this matter to the organization or have significance a year from now?

When Good Intentions Go Wrong

Ego Trap 5 can show itself in many forms, whether it's a leader with big ideas who wants them implemented immediately regardless of the team's current workload or the impatient boss who gives directives a few levels down the chain of command rather than working with a direct report. The intentions may be good—whether to keep the company on the cutting edge or to get tasks done quickly—but the fallout downstream often undermines the original worthy intentions. Some of the most common situations in which downstream impact can be felt are when leaders:

- Shift priorities on a whim or treat everything on their mind as a top priority
- Frequently change strategic direction ("initiatives du jour")
- Assign "simple" tasks that are actually time and resource intensive

- Level jump—that is, give assignments or directives to those further
  down the chain of command rather than to direct reports (just like
  Craig in Ego Trap 4)
- Assign projects without deadlines and then react with urgency or
  disappointment when they are not done on the leader's time line

I can still remember a time early in my career when I was the cocon-
spirator with a leader who was blind to his downstream impact. As the
well-meaning leader level jumped down to me, I fell into the same trap
because I was blind to it too.

I was a junior-level individual contributor working at a distribution company. My job was to deliver leadership training, so my path
crossed with Burke, the president of our company, who was four pay
grades above me. Burke was an intense but soft-spoken man with a keen
interest in professional development. Because his family had started the
company, he reached his role of president while still quite young, in his
mid-thirties. He routinely invited employees to have lunch with him as
a way to hear their ideas and avoid losing touch with the front line (Ego
Trap 7).

When I was eventually invited to have lunch with Burke, I was quite
nervous, unsure how to handle a one-on-one meeting with the president. I wondered how I would ever come up with anything interesting enough to say. Over lunch that day, Burke started by asking me a
lot of questions about my career and past employers. We discussed my
career history, best leadership development practices from my former
work experience, and my initial impressions of the company as a new
employee. Burke had a very conversational style, used a lot of direct eye
contact, and was an amazing listener. Because of our age proximity and
Burke's ability to put me at ease, I wasn't as intimidated as I thought I
would be. In fact, we had a great conversation, ending with his suggestion that on my upcoming business trip to Portland, I should be sure to
stop by and introduce myself to the distribution center manager there,

who was one of three women, out of twenty-five in the company, to hold that role. Burke was quite impressed with her and thought she could be a good internal contact for me, as she was a great example of a highly functional leader to use in my training programs.

I left the meeting full of enthusiasm and excitement, proud of myself for getting through a meeting with someone at Burke's level and eager to meet the female distribution center manager. The next day, I called her and mentioned that I would be in the area in the coming weeks and, if she could spare thirty minutes to meet, I would be most grateful. I told her that Burke had suggested the meeting and had spoken very highly of her. Now, recall that Burke was the president of the company and I was four levels below him on the food chain. I am sure you can imagine what happened next...

The distribution center manager called my boss's boss's boss—the SVP of Human Resources —to ask why Burke, the president of the company, would suggest that I, an HR representative, meet with her? And was there another agenda at work, meaning, should she be worried about something? My boss's boss's boss called my boss's boss, asking all the same questions. By the time it got back to me, I was on the phone with my boss on a Saturday morning with her screaming at me at the top of her lungs, "You've really blown it now! Who do you think you are, just scheduling a meeting with someone at her level? Why didn't you come and ask my permission?" I could barely respond to her verbal barrage and finally squeaked out, "I was just trying to follow Burke's advice..." She exploded. "You don't work for Burke. You work for *me*! From now on, everything you do and every move you make must be cleared by me! How do you think it feels for me to be the last one to hear about this from two levels up?! How do you think it felt for the DC manager to hear that Burke was sending someone in from HR to check on her?!"

For some business owners or entrepreneurs, it may be hard to understand why the DC manager reacted that way, but this is common corporate-America CYA behavior. I don't necessarily think that my boss handled the situation in the best way, but she was right, of course. It was a hard lesson for me to learn. Thinking back on how naïve I was about corporate politics, I realize that I completely mishandled the whole episode. It was a simple suggestion made by a very powerful man in the company, but the downstream impact had huge consequences for all of us. I was not allowed to see that DC manager on that trip. And Burke never heard about it and never followed up with me. It was a classic case of level jumping and, for Burke, a clueless cannonball dive into Ego Trap 5 that pulled me innocently into its potentially career-limiting wake. Can you imagine how much time and energy was spent by those above me sorting this out before the impact finally hit me in the face on a Saturday morning?

Whether it's a case of an egotistical leader who wants what he wants when he wants it or a well-intentioned suggestion from the president for a junior associate to call a high-level distribution center manager, every move the leader makes has a downstream impact, yet the leader may not even realize it. As employees down the line respond to the leader's requests with diligence, processing any negative fallout in the shadows, the leader may not see or hear how hard it is to deliver on these requests or recognize the disruptive impact of his behavior. As a result, the pattern repeats itself. It takes EQ—self-awareness, empathy, and self-control—to break the cycle.

YOU KNOW YOU'VE FALLEN INTO
EGO TRAP 5 IF:

- You routinely ask people to help you with a task, though it isn't their job, because you know they will get it done.
- You never hear "No" in answer to a request and are rarely asked to negotiate a deadline.
- You call last minute-meetings, assuming that everyone will clear their calendar for you, and they all show up.

- Before making a requested change, you don't consider how easy or difficult it will be to accomplish at *someone else's* level.
- You allow things to fall completely off the grid, then suddenly request an update.

The Battle of Ego vs. EQ

When operating from a place of ego, it's easy to fall into Trap 5. Ego says, "I have needs and my team will meet them." Ego says, "When I have an idea, I should have others implement it." Ego thinks about itself and doesn't notice the impact of its actions on everyone else. Ego doesn't pause to reflect on how others might perceive its behaviors.

In contrast, EQ says, "My team has needs too, and I will consider them when making my own known." EQ also signals the leader to consider the impact of making impulsive or last-minute requests on others in the group, recognizing that people have their own responsibilities to juggle. EQ reminds the leader that treating employees with respect breeds respect for the leader, whereas trampling on others can lead to weakened support and loyalty.

A Vacation Day or a Nightmare?

When leaders get too wrapped up in their own needs and perspectives, it's easy to forget that everyone on the team has needs too —and has other responsibilities. That happened for one of my clients, Meredith, the business owner of an insurance agency, who had a week's ski vacation scheduled with her family. She came home midweek, however, after one of her college-aged children broke a bone on the slopes. Suddenly, with Thursday and Friday open on her schedule, Meredith became giddy with the idea that she could catch up on work that had been piling up. She picked up the phone and dialed her director of HR, Claire. "Hey, I have a stack of things I'd like to turn over to you," Meredith explained.

"Can you come to my house tomorrow so we can spend the day catching up on all of this?" Claire rolled her eyes—not that Meredith ever saw it. Instead, Meredith found a helpful member of her executive team at her door the next day. Although Claire had a full schedule for Thursday and Friday of that week, she cleared it as best she could and slogged over to the boss's house the following day as requested. Like many direct reports, when the boss called, Claire rallied.

Could Claire have set some boundaries here or responded differently? Absolutely, and I encouraged her to do so in our coaching work together. Yet Meredith showed a lack of empathy, not once stopping to ask herself what Claire might already have on her schedule. It was almost as if Meredith projected her own empty schedule onto Claire, with an attitude of "I'm free so everyone must be free." Meredith came across as self-centered and unaware ("ego" and "clueless" often travel as a pair). Her intentions were good—keep the organization moving forward— but they were not filtered through the lens of emotional intelligence. If they had been, Meredith would have level-set the priority of the meeting against Claire's priorities and followed her request with the caveat that Claire could certainly decline if her schedule didn't allow the last-minute change. It would then be up to Claire to be honest about how much time she could spare—maybe an hour, or maybe nothing until her regularly scheduled meeting with Meredith the following week. But Claire would only be likely to do this if Meredith first gave Claire a way out, knowing that employees don't like to say no to the boss.

As the big cheese (or the "mucky-muck," as my boss referred to Burke), it's easy to forget how hard it is for people to say no to you. Yet you should never underestimate the magnitude of your communication and your power. Your team does not want to let you down, and they don't know the difference between your high priority and low priority unless you make it clear to them. If you make a request of your people, rest assured it immediately becomes their top priority, superseding all other tasks from lower down in the chain of command, regardless of how important or incidental your request actually is. So, instead of following up after a client meeting as planned, your team member might spend time with you creating the agenda for next week's staff meeting. Or, rather than making important new sales calls, she is stuck reviewing all the details of the missed shipment report with you. In contexts like these, it becomes ever clearer how a leader's requests can interfere with the organization's larger priorities.

It helps to be sensitive about other people's time. When you make requests that require adding tasks to team members' plates, are you mindful of the time required to complete the tasks and sensitive to the real workloads and schedules of the people around you? Do you invite people to give you a realistic sense of the time and resources they need and then set reasonable expectations everyone can agree upon? Or do you just steamroll?

EQ Antidote: Recognizing, Reading, and Responding

If ego has the leader thinking "the team is here to serve me," then EQ has the leader thinking the converse: "I am here to serve the team." In practice, it is a blend of these two approaches that helps get things done in an organization, but the other-directed, EQ-related mind-set can ensure that the leader never steps too far in the wrong direction toward that unwanted fall into Ego Trap 5.

Staying away from Trap 5 begins with exercising self awareness. The goal is to get good at *recognizing* when your ego is leading the way, causing you to instinctively make requests or engage in behaviors that you have not fully thought through in terms of possible downstream impact. If you have the urge to pitch a new strategy to your team, act on advice given in the latest business book, or hand out bonuses just because it *feels* right, notice this instinctive feeling and, instead of acting on it, pause and reflect on whether it is truly the right course of action—first, for yourself, and then for your team and organization.

Next, it's time to *read* the environment and exercise some empathy.

How will your request or the big idea that you're thinking about implementing affect your employees? Will it move the organization forward or disrupt work flow? Where would you rank your request or idea in terms of other organizational priorities? Is your ego leading the way or are you truly onto something important?

When you are ready to *respond*, keep your self-control at the ready. If, after looking both within and outside yourself, you still feel justified introducing your new idea, making a request, or engaging in a particular behavior, do so with sensitivity to everyone else. This may mean calling a meeting with your executive team to get their input and perspectives before rolling out a new idea. Or it may mean that when making your requests you acknowledge the required time outlay and give others enough time to shift around priorities. Or maybe you simply ask, "How does that work for you?"

When you use EQ rather than allowing your ego to reflexively lead the way, you may abandon some ideas and initiatives; others will be rolled out with pacing and consideration. That's good news for everyone as you maximize work flow and your best ideas get implemented in a way that works for the whole team.

BEWARE OF LEVEL JUMPING

A big no-no when it comes to Ego Trap 5 is level jumping—skipping past your direct reports and making requests directly to an employee somewhere further down in the chain of command. This is not to say that a leader should not be in dialogue with all levels of employees, but when the leader starts delegating work to anyone and everyone, it can become a problem. Some leaders fall into this trap out of impatience, giving in to the urge to assign work to the person they think is most likely to get it done the way they want. Other times, leaders make offhanded requests or suggestions to someone other than a direct report because that person just happens to be in front of them. While it may represent only a casual statement from the leader's perspective, the person who receives it may feel obligated to "jump to" and assign the task the highest priority. No one is going to put the CEO or president's request at the *bottom* of his to-do list, after all, and it's likely, out of respect for the leader, that the employee will not volunteer information about the impact your request will have on his schedule. So beware of your downstream impact! When you level jump, you can:

- Force employees to shuffle priorities to accommodate your needs (whether it's appropriate or not) and prevent people from working on their responsibilities
- Create mistrust—doing things out of order or being unpredictable can make others wary of you
- Put employees in the awkward position of serving two masters— their direct boss as well as you
- Muddy the lines of authority and decision-making rights, challenging formal reporting lines
- Make people feel undervalued and cause them to disengage when you sidestep them instead of having them do the work you hired them to do

Instead of level jumping, plan to work through your direct reports. By enlisting them in your initiatives, you build stronger trust with your team. They know what is going on firsthand, and you develop greater bench strength in successive leaders for the long term.

In a Nutshell

When you are a top-level executive or founder of the company, it's easy to have a blind spot regarding your downstream impact: you may not have any advisors to give you feedback, and the masses in the organization—even your executive team—may silently defer to you.

Chances are that they will never let on, at least directly, to the disruptive effects of your decisions, initiatives, requests, and behavior. Add to that your busy schedule and daily demands as an executive, and it becomes easy to be blind to your impact on those downstream.

For the senior executive who regularly communicates the belief that "my needs take priority over everyone else's," problems may occur. Employees can start to feel disrespected and become disgruntled. The leader may become the butt of a few jokes around the office or, worse, set himself up to be undermined by others as they disengage and fail to alert the leader to possible trouble, or even set the leader up for failure. No one wants to work for a dictator, even a benevolent one.

For the leader with an ego-based outlook, it becomes all too easy to make requests that are unfair intrusions on team members' time, that confuse priorities, that lower morale, and that chip away at the leader's own credibility. Instead, by keeping your EQ wits about you, you gain the tools needed to ensure that your team really listens when you have a legitimate new initiative for consideration. You gain credibility points for acknowledging the impact of your requests on others, and you maintain motivation. In the end, you serve your team and the organization by keeping your workforce energized and focused on a clear strategic direction that advances the cause.

APPLYING THE THREE R'S

Recognize when you are about to engage in behavior that could have a disruptive impact on your team and ask yourself how this meets your personal needs versus those of others in the organization (self-awareness). Be cognizant of how you are communicating any necessary changes to your team and why these changes are happening. Are you tying these changes to a clear and stable strategic direction or giving the impression that you're onto another initiative du jour?

Read what is going on with your team right now (empathy), and consider how your behavior might affect their day-to-day workflow and understanding of the organization's strategic direction. Can you step beyond your own needs and assess what the team and organization need?

Respond only after thinking through the downstream impact of your potential actions (self-control). Does your latest idea represent a personal whim, or is it truly the best path for your organization? Ask yourself whether this idea or plan really requires the urgency you give it. Will it take more resources, time, and disruption than you originally thought?

Ego Trap 6

Underestimating How Much You Are Being Watched

Whether it's the time you arrive at work, the way you sign your e-mails, or the accolades you give or neglect to give to team members at the year-end party—in all these ways, and many more, your employees are watching you. While many leaders know in a general sense that others are observing and reacting to them, they are often surprised by the degree of detail on which employees zero in. "I understand your pet peeve is semicolons," I recently shared with a CEO client of mine, who chuckled with surprise that people had noticed. "People are talking about that?" he asked. Yep, people are talking about that.

As noted by Michael Porter and Nitin Nohria in Harvard Business Press's *Handbook of Leadership Theory and Practice*, "although the power of the CEO's position is often overestimated, in one respect it is sometimes underestimated—and that is its symbolic significance (Pondy, 1983; Pfeffer, 1981). CEOs we have studied are often surprised by how much their behavior is scrutinized and the symbolic messages people derive from these behaviors."[1] When the leader makes an off-handed comment about hating semicolons, his team may interpret that as a directive on writing style for company e-mails. When the leader points out an employee for bringing lunch from home—while the rest of the team orders in—the employee may quickly calculate that, to fit into this culture, she has to give up her healthy midday meals and up her lunch budget. Simple statements and actions often take on great weight when it's the leader who's making them. Individuals want to please the leader, out of deference and respect, and because they often perceive their jobs as depending on it. So they take each and every word and action by the leader seriously, even when the leader says something off-handed or even in jest.

If folks quietly tell one another not to send the boss e-mails with too many semicolons after they've heard him complain about them, as they did at my client's company, just imagine how they react to more significant behavior on the part of the leader. The following story of a CEO and CFO at a software company reveals the more extreme end of the spectrum.

It was the weekend of the big corporate retreat. Everyone attending was excited to take a break from the office routine and participate in the global sales meeting at a luxurious California hotel. The CEO/founder and the CFO, good friends, hoped to lead the way in relaxing and having some fun. Unfortunately, they ended up pushing their normal raucous style at these events over the edge.

The third night at the resort, after hours of drinking, they recruited a small group of colleagues, including three female employees left at the hotel bar, to sneak outside to swim in the pool. A series of dares resulted in the CFO climbing a palm tree to break into the locked pool area where the group eventually ended up skinny-dipping. Because it was the middle of the night, the leaders thought they wouldn't be found out. But, unbeknownst to the revelers, their employees' hotel rooms faced the pool. The fact that the group was hardly quiet meant that it didn't take long for the executives to be outed.

What might have been a funny story had the group been college students became an HR and PR nightmare for the publicly traded company. The repercussions were major: word of the bad behavior spread like wildfire, first through the attendees of the meeting, then back to those in the organization at home. After the group returned to the office, the three women involved were fired (one woman later sued for wrongful termination). A disgruntled employee posted an account of the incident, as seen from his hotel window, on the web. Eventually, the director of marketing and the HR director, neither of whom was involved, resigned on principle, feeling that the way the situation was handled by the executives, during and after the fact, was beyond inappropriate. And what became of the executives who led the charge? Well, they fared a little better, at least initially.

The CEO and CFO retained their jobs, as cronies on the board were unwilling to fire them. This was in spite of the fact that the executives did not deliver a formal explanation or make an apology, instead remaining silent on the entire incident. It's no surprise that employee morale plummeted and respect for the leaders was nil. And though the CEO and CFO seemed at first glance to emerge unscathed, the incident clearly caused irreparable damage. Their executive team had been routed by the incident, and those who stayed on the team now had unhealthy leverage and bargaining power that could undermine the CEO and CFO's ability to lead.

Sure, these executives had the right to act in any way they chose— it's always an option to handle oneself inappropriately. But is that the example these leaders really wanted to set? If their direct reports acted with similar thoughtless behavior, how could these leaders legitimately reprimand, discipline, or say anything at all to correct it? Bad behavior on the part of the leader undermines his ability to hold other people accountable for their behavior.

Whether it's a case of simple disdain for semicolons or a case of extremely poor judgment after a night of carousing, the leader's behavior is always under scrutiny. Make no mistake about it, everyone watches what you do. As leader of the organization, your behavior—for good or for ill—is the primary model according to which everyone else acts. People will follow your manners, conduct, and writing or presentation style. It's not a bad thing, necessarily. What is a bad thing is to underestimate or abuse this power.

Ego Trap 6 is triggered when leaders fail to appreciate the degree to which their behaviors are being observed by others. This failure can cause leaders to engage in behavior that privately may seem innocuous, but when displayed publicly has a negative impact on the team. Even *neglecting to engage* in certain behaviors—for example, ignoring another's transgression or not acknowledging a team achievement—can have a negative influence on the team.

That almost sounds a little bit like Ego Trap 5 (being blind to your downstream impact), where the leader engages in behavior, often impulsive or unplanned, that has a disruptive effect on the team or organization. But it's different. Underestimating being watched (Trap 6) is about thinking you can do things behind closed doors, whereas downstream impact (Trap 5) is about overt, open requests. Underestimating being watched is about how magnified your behaviors are in the eyes of your followers, whereas downstream impact is about how disruptive your behaviors are in the eyes of your followers. With Ego Trap 6, it's a matter of being aware of the influence you have over others through the behavior you exhibit day in and day out.

If there is something you aren't happy about in your organization, it's time to hold up a mirror. Remember, you model the desired behavior at your organization. In what ways are your people mimicking your behavior? Are there disadvantages to the culture you've created? What behaviors do you want reinforced and perpetuated? As a leader, by exhibiting those behaviors for your organization, you have tremendous power to design every aspect of the culture and encourage others to follow your lead.

A Closer Look at the Trap

Why is it so important to appreciate how much you are being watched as a leader? It's not just a matter of playing the part because that makes the organization "look good" or because it retains your credibility—although those are both important issues. It's that you as the leader are the ultimate behavioral model for the organization. People learn what is acceptable and appropriate by seeing how *you* conduct yourself.

As leadership development experts, Jim Kouzes and Barry Posner have shown with the Leadership Practices Inventory (LPI), their extensively studied and validated instrument for measuring the five areas most important to being a successful leader, modeling is an essential piece of effective leadership. Kouzes and Posner call it "modeling the way" and break it down like this:

> Leaders establish principles concerning the way people (constituents, peers, colleagues, and customers alike) should be treated and the way goals should be pursued. They create standards of excellence and then set an example for others to follow...; they put up signposts when people are unsure of where to go or how to get there.[2]

Whether it's in the area of helping individuals navigate "complex change that can overwhelm...and stifle action" or to "unravel bureaucracy when it impedes action," Kouzes and Posner remind us of just how many areas the leader can influence by modeling exemplary behavior.

Ego Trap 6 is a reminder to leaders to be aware of their profound influence on the organization. Although single incidents can have their impact, repeated failures to appreciate how closely one is being watched can create more widespread problems. For example, at the software company where the skinny-dipping incident took place, that type of inappropriate behavior was not an isolated event. The CEO and CFO had created such a hard-drinking, anything-goes culture at these annual conferences that employees seemed to compete to see who could act craziest. I once witnessed this firsthand when, at one of these events, a male employee picked up a female coworker, threw her over his shoulder in a fireman's carry, and started walking her out of the bar despite her vigorous protests and attempts to free herself. This individual was his coworker, though onlookers would have thought she was his kid sister or a girlfriend. Did this employee stop to think about how anyone else would perceive his behavior? And why would he have reason to worry about his unprofessional behavior? The CEO and CFO were across the barroom acting just as crazy. Message received: anything goes around here. That's *influence*.

While a leader's negative influence could be as egregious as that of the skinny-dipping executives, more commonly it's routine and subtle. Sometimes it's the CEO who is generous with criticism and sparse with praise at executive meetings. His direct reports may simply turn around and throw that same criticism onto their own teams, because that's become the norm at the company. You can rest assured that the new norm will be copied by anyone bucking for a promotion.

It may involve an even more subtle behavior, for example, the executive who likes to type on his computer while people are talking to him or the leader who checks her phone while others are presenting. Then there's the executive who's not harsh with criticism but who in haste misses an opportunity to deliver appropriate praise or connect with folks, a sort of sin of omission. I learned of just such a situation when recently speaking with Christine, an employee of a specialty health-care organization that operated in several locations.

On the day we met, Christine explained to me that the CEO had visited her site that morning, as he was being filmed for a promotional video. The video producers wanted to use an operational center instead of the CEO's office, to show him in action. I asked Christine how it went, and she said, "Well, the filming went pretty well. They got everything they needed with minimal disruption to our operations. But..." She hesitated.

"But what?" I asked.

"It was just a little disappointing," she responded, "because as soon as the CEO was done filming he left immediately. We were hoping he might stop and say hello to our frontline employees. We won 'Community of the Year' and it would have been nice if he could have acknowledged everyone for all their hard work."

I cringed inside, knowing the significant damage this leader had just brought upon himself. I know this CEO, and he is not any sort of egomaniac. He has worked with a coach for years and is typically very attuned to his role and the company culture, but this was a missed opportunity based purely, I believe, on a blind spot. The CEO probably had a jam-packed schedule that day and needed to get somewhere else quickly; nonetheless, he missed a prime opportunity to engage his hardest-working, highest-performing group of fully engaged employees. His hasty departure may also have been based on a benign, even kind, but inaccurate assumption that he would get out of their hair and not disrupt their business further.

No matter the real reason, the company's frontline people saw every move the CEO made, and in the absence of any other communication from him to refute it, they drew their own negative conclusions. They felt invisible to him. "What the CEO shows an interest in," Porter and Nohria tell us, "is quickly interpreted as being important, while what the CEO consciously or unconsciously neglects can be as readily interpreted as being unimportant." That certainly was the case for this company on that day.

One thing is clear: the team learns by watching you. In particular, they learn:

- Which parts of the company are most and least "important"
- What is acceptable and unacceptable behavior
- Which rules must be followed and which can be broken
- What the "real" company values are
- How high your self-awareness and integrity are, based on how congruent your actions are with your words

Leaders who fall into Ego Trap 6 are conducting themselves as if they are working behind closed doors, unseen by others, when in fact the opposite is true. Not only are others always watching the leader, they are interpreting the leader's every move and using it as hard data to guide their own behavior. Regardless of intent, the leader's *interpreted* behavior becomes the truth. As a result, leaders need to think of themselves as a sort of "chief culture officer" who sets the tone for the entire organization. Leaders can't then settle for an approach of "Don't do as I do, do as I say."

We have all seen hypocritical leaders who model certain negative behaviors, thus setting expectations for acceptable conduct, but are then seen speaking out against the very things they themselves do. The reality is that leaders have to walk the talk because people will mimic them—their own executive team, the direct reports of the executive team, and employees all through the organization.

YOU KNOW YOU HAVE FALLEN INTO
EGO TRAP 6 IF:

- You think that there are different rules for executives than for everyone else.
- At a company function you sit with your small circle of peers or direct reports instead of using it as an opportunity to meet employees you don't know.
- You believe it's okay to behave like everyone else at company meetings because it makes you "one of the guys."
- You chronically put scheduling priorities over opportunities to spend time with employees.

The Battle of Ego vs. EQ

Whereas the ego can make it easy to focus on self—and forget how others see you and interpret your behavior—a sharpened EQ reminds you to step into other people's shoes and observe yourself objectively for a time. What is it that others see when they look at you? Do they see a leader who runs chronically late for meetings or who exempts himself from company policy and values? Or, instead, do they see a leader who embodies company values, respects and honors employees, and understands that even little actions by a leader make an important statement about the organization and its culture? Maybe setting the cultural tone and creating standards is something you've mistakenly delegated to line leaders, thinking this makes you exempt.

With Ego Trap 6, it may be a case of being busy and forgetting to connect with the frontline employees, as happened with the health-care CEO who left the operational center after filming, or it may be a greater arrogance. (If you ask Christine, the distinction was moot.) Either way, the ego takes over, pushing the needs of the team or the organization into the shadows in favor of one's own.

A Power for Good

As we saw from the work of Kouzes and Posner, and as Harvard Business Press authors Porter and Nohria point out, a leader's behavior can also be a force for good in the organization. In particular, "CEOs can leverage the symbolic power of presence to send powerful messages about desirable behavior."[3] I saw this positive influence early in my career when I worked as a customer service manager at high-end apparel retailer Nordstrom.

Whereas some business owners are guilty of exempting themselves from company policy or walling themselves off in mahogany-lined boardrooms, the second generation of Nordstrom leaders at the helm when I worked there—"Mr. John," "Mr. Jim," and "Mr. Bruce" Nordstrom—made it clear through their behaviors that they were both accessible and engaged. For example, their corporate offices are upstairs and directly above the downtown Seattle flagship store rather than off-site, and when the store would get busy around the holidays, these gentlemen would walk onto the floor and start helping customers. In addition, they had set a company policy that no phone calls would be screened, so that customers and vendors could always get access to whomever they needed. Sure enough, Mr. Jim, Mr. John, and Mr. Bruce all answered their own phones. I recall customers being able to reach them with ease. Message received: do as I do. Also of note, as the next generation of Nordstroms started working in the family business, these folks did not leapfrog the rest of us into an executive suite, but instead were assigned to work in the stockroom or on the sales floor, then to management, progressing up the ranks as all other store employees were required to do.

Jim, John, and Bruce lived their company policies and values—and that signaled to the rest of us how important these values were. In addition, they sent the message that we were all in this together. As we noticed these leaders' presence, we felt motivated to do our best work. For years, Nordstrom had the lowest turnover in the retail industry and was known for its excellent customer service. I'm sure it was in part due to the Nordstrom leaders' appreciation for how they would be viewed by their employees and customers—self-awareness and empathy combined.

Just as ego says, "I am special," EQ reminds the leader, "I have a special role to play and I am watched." Where ego says, "I can do as I please without affecting others," EQ says, "My own behavior is my primary tool of influence on the group." When EQ is activated, there is a clear awareness of how self affects others that helps the leader to make the kinds of choices needed to avoid Ego Trap 6. EQ tells the executive to leave the late-night party at the conference at 11 p.m., not 2 a.m. It reminds the leader to pop onto the factory floor and say hello to the individuals who won last year's quality award before rushing off to make the corporate jet. It makes the executive think twice before sending out an e-mail to the team at 3 a.m., knowing that they might interpret it as a sign that the boss is losing sleep over an issue, not that she got back from a late-night flight and is catching up on work. EQ reminds the leader that his every move is carefully watched, then interpreted, and often magnified.

SIX QUESTIONS TO ASK WHEN AVOIDING TRAP 6

Even executives with strong EQ sometimes fall into Ego Trap 6. Here are six simple questions to ask yourself occasionally, to make sure you don't take an unexpected slip into this pitfall.

1. At staff meetings do I follow my impulse to act like one of the guys, or do I maintain a more professional tone?
2. When I go to company events, do I stick with the people I know well or do I get out of my comfort zone and mingle?
3. Are there areas of my work where I preach one thing but do another?
4. When it comes to company procedures, do I hold myself account-able or do I act as if I'm above the rules?
5. Do I behave pretty much the same way I did earlier in my career or have I matured into the leader my people need me to be?
6. Have I visited operations lately during a second or graveyard shift?

EQ Antidote: Recognizing, Reading, and Responding

So, how do you ensure that you don't fall into Ego Trap 6? The best safeguard is to stay tuned to the way you are being perceived by others— that is, to apply your *social* self awareness. Instead of underestimating how much you are being watched, begin to appreciate that you *are* being watched—to the *n*th degree—and practice putting yourself in other people's shoes so you can better understand how your behaviors may be perceived. You can use the three Rs to help you stay on track.

First, *recognize* the behaviors and choices you engage in (self-awareness) that may be judged and interpreted by others. Are you setting a positive and professional tone at meetings, or are you a little too casual or even sarcastic? Which departments are you staying connected to and which, if any, are you neglecting? Have you done an employee morale study to determine what traits and behavior your employees value most? Just as you size up others and make mental judgments, any area of your leadership and personal conduct is ripe for judgment or interpretation. Are you paying close attention to the way you act and interact so you stay aware of your potential influence on others?

This may be a good time to address a couple of objections you may have at this point, namely the issues of privacy and fairness, as in "I don't live in a fishbowl. I'm entitled to be left alone and not be judged" and "I can't control what everybody thinks. It's completely unfair to interpret my behavior in ways I don't intend." These are reasonable expectations for anyone—unless of course everybody in the same room sees you as their boss, leader, guiding light, and hope for the future. If you want to lead effectively, and if you've read this far you must, then understand what people need from a leader and be that for them.

Now back to using the three Rs to avoid Trap 6.

Given that you are being watched, and that your behaviors as the leader hold great sway over the group, it's important to take the time to *read* others (i.e., have empathy). How might your behaviors be perceived by your team and your people in a given situation? You don't need to be psychic, just look for cues and helpful information. What body language and facial expressions do people have when you speak? What comments, complaints, or concerns do you hear from your direct reports or the peanut gallery? Are you being mindful and paying attention enough to assess what the immediate situation calls for from you? If you are having trouble reading a situation, it's okay to ask for information, too. In a one-on-one meeting, spend time asking questions to understand where the other person is coming from. In a group setting, note nonverbal cues, such as body language, being displayed to help you get a better read. It can also be helpful to work with a coach, who can offer you an outside perspective and help you empathize with others. Coaches give new sight where there are currently blind spots.

With a better awareness of your own behaviors and insight into the ways they may be perceived by others, you can make adjustments (i.e., use self-control). Sometimes, this may mean backtracking, like making an apology for inappropriate past behavior (like skinny-dipping at the annual conference or chronically cancelling meetings). Other times, it may mean adjusting future behavior, like scheduling an appointment to visit frontline workers you missed on your last site visit or putting a special thank-you to these workers in the upcoming newsletter. Even better, use your self-awareness, empathy, and self-control to catch yourself, heading off incidents that can have a negative influence on your people so that you're making deliberate, proactive choices to model good behavior from the start. That being said, it's rarely too late to say, "I'm sorry" or to give thanks after the fact. As a leader, you are allowed to be human; your EQ is there to help you make the best impression you can on others, whether from the start or to recover from lapses in behavior or judgment. People aren't drawn to perfection; they are inspired and influenced by vulnerability, humility, and courage.

You may remember Marty from Ego Trap 5—he's the fiery Latino business founder who had to work on letting go of control. As it turns out, Marty was very human, and also had some work to do in order to avoid Ego Trap 6. Along with his passionate personality came a tendency to speak casually and off the cuff at staff meetings. Unfortunately, Marty often lacked the self-monitoring skills to filter his poor behavior. At one meeting, he blurted out, "Aww, now you're just kissing ass!" as he observed one individual offer to help someone higher in the chain of command.

Several people in the room cringed as Marty descended from the role of president to rowdy frat boy. First, the tone was crass and unprofessional, not the ideal leadership model for his people. Second, even if Marty hadn't cursed, the fact that he was vocally judging the social interaction between two group members made others feel uncomfortable. "What might he say about one of us next?" they thought.

In fact, at another point during the meeting Marty pitted two employees against each other by announcing, "So, what you're saying, Sherry, is that Antonio [who was sitting right there] is being a jerk." The signs of low self-awareness were evident there as well. The result? Marty came across as clueless, impulsive, and unpredictable. His comments were more suited to hanging at the bar with his buddies than at a meeting of employees who were making note of his every move. Marty, of course, didn't mean any harm, but his behavior caused damage. Some folks in the group grew more distant from Marty as they lost respect for him, while others learned that it was okay to speak with blunt and impulsive familiarity, taking potshots at others in the group, seemingly without consequence. Like Marty's ego, consequences were all over the place at that meeting.

Could Marty recover? Fortunately, yes. Even though he had more than one ego blind spot to manage, he, like everyone, had the capacity to increase his emotional intelligence. As indicated by Daniel Goleman, EQ is a behavior that can be learned.[4] Kouzes and Posner add to that fact the important notion that "Leadership is not about personality; it's about behavior—an observable set of skills and abilities."[5] If Marty could begin *acting* with more emotional intelligence, then he would become more effective as a leader.

In my debrief meeting with Marty, I started by quoting verbatim what he'd said about "kissing ass." Since he didn't have the initial *self-awareness* to notice that behavior, I simply held up a mirror for him. Next, I encouraged Marty to think about how his statement about Antonio might have appeared to others and how it might have made that specific employee feel (*empathy*). After recognizing his own behavior and reading the reaction of the employee (Marty recalled that Antonio had started blushing), Marty decided it was best to apologize to Antonio for making the comment. Antonio responded well to the apology, surprised but pleased that Marty had taken the time and had the humility to acknowledge his mistake and make the situation right.

Marty also made a commitment to practice more presence of mind and discipline at future meetings. It wouldn't be easy, as it was far more natural for Marty to speak without monitoring himself; however, where there is a motivation and commitment, behavior can change.[6] Over time, new habits can be built, like muscles that are strengthened with use. For example, with a sincere desire to change and regular practice, Marty has in fact strengthened his own EQ "muscles" and improved his ability to monitor himself, read what's going on for others, and act accordingly. As a result, he's falling into Ego Traps 5 and 6 less and less.

It's a lesson that leader Rick—who we will meet again when we discuss Ego Trap 8—knows well. As the largest employer in his small Midwestern town, Rick had long ago discovered at the grocery store, restaurants, and the bank that people know he's the company president. As a result, after picking me up at the airport for a coaching visit and giving me a friendly hug, Rick (who was married) said, "I'm probably going to hear about it at work tomorrow that I was seen hugging a blonde. I don't know these people, but they all know me." And he was right: many in the community knew who he was, and word of his behavior and whereabouts often trickled back into the office.

Like Rick, as a senior executive you have star status. Although you may feel hidden away in your ivory tower, what you say and do holds weight. In fact, you can assume it to be magnified tenfold. By never underestimating the degree to which people are watching you, you can use your influence consciously and for the good of the organization. Once you truly understand the weight of your influence, even when demonstrated in small ways—like sitting with a table of administrative staff at the holiday party or volunteering alongside junior folks at a community event you've sponsored—you will discover that simple decisions about your own behavior will go a long way toward creating a positive culture for the organization.

In a Nutshell

When you're an executive, people pay attention to you. Whether it's what you say, who you talk to, or how you dress for the office, the team and the organization will have a read on it. They won't always interpret your behavior correctly, but interpret it they will. Are you doing everything within your power to be the ultimate role model for your company? Are you using your behavior as a force for positive influence?

While it can feel comfortable to operate under the premise that you are just one of the guys, the reality is that as a leader you are the paragon for your organization. People look to you for guidance, validation, and culture setting. How you act, in each and every moment, has tremendous influence over your team, your employees, and the organization. To avoid Ego Trap 6, aim to have the situational awareness to recognize when your behaviors matter most and to read what others need from you. When leadership matters, and it often does, choose your behaviors as if the organization's success depended on them.

APPLYING THE THREE R'S

Recognize the ways in which your conduct, manners, and habits permeate the organization's culture—both good and bad (self-awareness). What serves your organization well? What doesn't? Many people will adopt your means and methods of getting business done, and this natural mimicry can be either positive or negative. So be a relentless quality and integrity inspector of yourself. Watch for any signs of exempt thinking or behaving as well as actions that convey mixed messages to the group.

Read the environment carefully. Generally the C-circle is pretty tight, or the business owner may be very close with the employees. Consider how much of what you see in others—what you like and dislike—is actually a reflection of you (empathy).

Respond only after evaluating the message your behavior will send to the organization (self-control). It's vital to know when you can't do today what you may have done in the past. You can also informally poll your most engaged employees or A-players for feedback on the ways—good and bad—that your work style is repeated by others throughout the organization.

Ego Trap 7

Losing Touch with the Frontline Experience

Picture this: the CEO of Subway sandwiches taking more than five minutes—three hundred long seconds—to make a foot-long sandwich while customers wait in line.[1] Or imagine Stephen Joyce, the CEO of Choice Hotels, sweating profusely as he struggles to stock a cleaning cart with supplies. "I am sweating like crazy, and all I seem to do is get behind," an exasperated Joyce once said under these circumstances.[2]

Maybe these images already strike a familiar chord for fans of CBS's *Undercover Boss*, where these and many other CEOs have been featured as they try to reengage with their frontline workers while working alongside them, incognito, as supposed trainees and newbies. The Emmy Award–winning reality TV series, averaging 17.7 million viewers, offers a treasure trove of stories of leaders who have fallen into Ego Trap 7, losing touch with the frontline experience after too many years away from it or perhaps never having been connected to it in the first place.[3]

Take, for example, American Seafoods Group's CEO, Bernt Bodal, who admits, "I haven't done this job [as a deckhand] in twenty-six years and it's maybe harder than I remembered."[4] Hooters's then-CEO Coby Brooks witnesses a restaurant manager being disrespectful to the female waitresses and notes, "The things I saw today...were inappropriate. They were wrong and I don't want any part of it...the way he approached the girls was not acceptable."[5] A moment of truth occurs for these executives as they begin to realize what they have been missing while leading from far above the front line, in the lofty ivory tower of the organization.

What might you learn by reengaging and considering your front line? As a senior executive, it is all too easy to become disconnected from the troops. The contrast between the frontline environment and the physical surroundings of the average executive—large, private offices, dining-room-sized conference tables, and private gyms or private jets—is one reason. Then consider the contrast in the nature, complexity, and seriousness of the work, such as conversations with peer executives, and, if you are part of a publicly traded company, shareholder meetings and appointments with analysts—and you'll realize how easy it is to forget what's going on beneath you. It is only by making a conscious effort to stay connected to the frontline experience that you can avoid Ego Trap 7. Otherwise, the trappings of your position will likely throw up blinders along the way that can disconnect you from your core business.

A Closer Look at the Trap

Whether it's the bank teller, factory worker, window washer, driller in the oil field, or the employee packaging products in the distribution center, there are frontline workers powering businesses around the globe. These individuals are touching your product or delivering your service every day, often interacting with your customers, shaping the customers' opinions about your brand and securing their future buying choices. Yet, the demands on you as a senior executive to be focused on investors, analysts, the board, or quarterly profits makes it easy for you to take your eye off the organizational culture and lose empathy for those who have to execute your plans.

Ego Trap 7 gets triggered when leaders are disconnected from what it's really like to work and be on the front line or floor, day after day. Leaders may also be disconnected from *the way their decisions and what they pay attention to* impact the people on the front line. For example, what might seem like a simple decision to reduce costs by eliminating the perk of company cell phones for certain employees could have a big impact on operations and morale.

Cutting the Smartphone Fat

As his company was going through a rough time, the CEO of a metal products manufacturer in the Southeast scrambled to find ways to cut costs. Buddy, the CEO, prided himself on his ability to run an efficient, lowest-cost operation. He wasn't afraid to act. So, given the company's recent downturn, he zeroed in on cell phones: anyone below a director level would no longer be provided a company smartphone.

On paper, the move seemed like a reasonable way to slash expenses. In practice, however, it made little sense: the managers and supervisors below the director level were the ones most often on the factory floor; their jobs required constant movement. They stopped seeing meeting time changes sent via e-mail, which they could no longer check on a company smartphone, and started missing important meetings. In addition, they couldn't be reached in real time to resolve issues related to the manufacturing line, which resulted in lost production time.

Meanwhile, the directors who retained their phones were the ones who worked mostly in the office and had constant access to a landline, a desktop computer, and their e-mail calendars. After pleas to change the policy fell on deaf ears, the most engaged employees started using their own personal smartphones for business use—which was against the company's policies. But they were so committed to doing their jobs well that they risked disciplinary action for violating the rules.

Buddy—clearly trying to make a logical decision—missed a key piece of information. Thinking smartphones were a privilege or status item, he acted without gathering feedback or paying a visit to the shop floor. If he had visited, he would likely have realized how essential smartphones were to his frontline supervisors and daily operations. Instead, his ego blind spots made life much more difficult for the group who spent little time at a desk, while offsetting smartphone costs for those in the company who actually had less need for the devices. "Crazy," said some employees. "Clueless and cheap," others would call Buddy behind his back. It took several months of minor chaos, as well as disruptions to other budget items, before the situation was finally corrected and reimbursements for smartphones were reinstated.

When leaders fall out of touch with the frontline experience and fail to check in with the troops on a regular basis, negative consequences like those faced by the metal products CEO can easily result. For example:

1. Valuable information on how the company can improve and increase its competitive advantage may get missed because these issues are often most evident at the front line. This is also where the greatest ideas are typically born.
2. Poor decisions are made because leaders cannot adequately anticipate the ripple effect of their decisions or behavior.
3. Leaders lose credibility with the workforce. People lose confidence in their leaders and question whether to follow them because they believe the leaders have no clue what is really going on in the company.

Losing touch with your front line, or even being perceived that way because of a lack of visibility, is a surefire way to lose both your credibility and your employee loyalty.

Why do leaders, many of whom got their start on the ground floor, sometimes lose touch as they ascend? Many have mopped those same floors and manned the same production lines. One would think this would make it nearly impossible to lose sight of their roots. Yet often they seem to suffer from the same hindsight blindness as many CEOs out there who came in as management and never worked a day in the trenches. Getting connected with those furthest below you takes some work and ongoing commitment.

By stepping out of the executive suite often enough to ensure you understand what's happening on the front line—since that's the heart-beat of the organization—you can keep your finger on the pulse of what employees need to be successful, see how they perceive your product or service, and discover the often hidden but most impactful opportunities for your organization to grow and prosper. You may also gain deeper insight into ways to better interact with the client or customer.

When we skim the outcomes of episodes of *Undercover Boss,* we see at a glance the kind of positive changes that leaders are able to make after reengaging their entry-level workforce. Here are some of the changes that these high-profile leaders instituted after spending time on the front line, changes with the potential to lift company morale, improve pro-ductivity, and help develop internal talent.

- After realizing how hard it was for employees to be out of touch with family members, American Seafoods Group's CEO Bernt Bodal created a company mandate to ensure Internet access across the company's fleet of boats.[6]
- After struggling to carve chickens all day long, Boston Market's chief brand officer, Sarah Bittorf, who is left-handed, committed to making the company's procedures easier for other lefties.[7]
- Subway's Don Fertman, chief development officer, discovered that the "sandwich artists" on the front line had "great ideas on how to make the business better," and pledged to start having individuals from corporate take time to work at actual Subway stores.[8]
- NASCAR's chief marketing officer, Steve Phelps, after discovering the passion of employees like pit crew members and paint rollers,

decided to create a council of employees—akin to NASCAR's existing council of fans—so these folks could provide valuable feedback and insight to upper management.[9]

The skeptics out there may be thinking, *that wasn't the work of the executives, that was what the scriptwriters and producers came up with to sell good TV.* If it's true, my response to that is, *why did it take a reality TV show to wake up the executives to the real needs of their companies?*

Without moments on the front line, leaders can easily become blind to what it's like for rank-and-file employees leading the charge from the front. What might you learn by reengaging and considering your front line?

Learning from the Customer-Service Experts

We can look to companies like Zappos, Nordstrom, and Disney for models on how to stay engaged with the front line. At successful retailer Zappos, CEO Tony Hsieh has a cubicle, not an office, and it is right in the middle of the floor with everyone else.[10] And just as Hsieh stays connected to his people through choices like this, he has also created a culture in which his people stay connected to the frontline experience of the customer. According to Hsieh: "Everyone that's hired, it doesn't matter what position—you can be an accountant, lawyer, software developer—goes through the exact same training as our call center reps. It's a four-week training program and then they're actually on the phone for two weeks taking calls from customers."[11] These are just a few examples of how Zappos is able to live out its mantra of "Be Humble," one of the company's core values. This sounds similar to the Nordstrom family, who ensures that employees get experience working at the lower ranks of the company before being promoted up the chain (see Ego Trap 6 for more information). Zappos, Nordstrom—and Disney—have all been recognized as leaders in the customer experience.

For example, Disney is very clear that the frontline *employee* experience directly impacts the frontline *customer* experience. It's likely no accident that Disney has made record numbers since the 2008 economic downturn, while other companies are still struggling to recover.[12] And Disney makes it look easy, whether through their amazing child recovery system or their FASTPASS program, which helps park guests avoid long lines.

I learned about the child recovery system several years ago the hard way, when my then three-year-old daughter vanished as we passed (with five adults in the group!) through a busy area of the park and came out the other side without her. It was terrifying. As our group of adults dispersed to look for her, a gentleman in plain clothes approached us and asked, "Have you lost a child?" When we said yes, he radioed to a Disney counterpart and responded to us within seconds, "We've got her." And in record time, considering the size of the sprawling park. Relief. Our group was able to enjoy the rest of our day, and Disney avoided a PR nightmare.

Later, I contemplated the experience and how the park staff had been able to locate my daughter so quickly. I was informed by a friend who worked at Disney that the company had studied the park and was highly aware of crowded spots where it was easy to lose children. They intentionally station plainclothes employees in those locations, specifically prepared to look out for and secure lost children before anyone unintended might be able to do so. Thankfully, they're also fairly astute at spotting panicked parents. So my quickly found child was no accident or anomaly, but instead a positive result of the Disney corporation staying in touch with the frontline experience.

Ironically, while most companies have a stated "open door policy," most executives are on their own floor, with a secure entrance or receptionist "guard dog." This reality only makes awareness of the front line even harder. Out of sight, out of mind. Yet Disney is *masterful* at not letting a disconnect happen—but it's not *magic*. Regular visits to the front line and a healthy dose of EQ can help ensure that any executive stays connected to frontline workers and the customer experience that they create.

YOU KNOW YOU'VE FALLEN INTO EGO TRAP 7 IF:

- You have employees come to your office for a meeting instead of going to theirs.
- You don't periodically spend time working alongside employees for a "day in the life" experience.
- You have employees working in locations you have never visited. (Anywhere in the *world* you ask? Yes, anywhere in the *world*.)
- You always fly first class or on the company jet, while your travel policy requires that all employees fly coach.

The Battle of Ego vs. EQ

Like all the traps described in this book, Ego Trap 7 is triggered when a leader's ego eclipses the useful safeguards of EQ: self-awareness, empathy, and self-control. Whereas ego says, "I'm too busy to spend time on the factory floor" or "I feel uncomfortable taking off my suit and making sandwiches next to my entry-level employees," EQ says "I want to spend time with the folks on the ground floor so I can get to know what they and the organization really need" or "It's okay to operate out of my element because in order to grow I need to do things that stretch my abilities and connect me to new areas of my business." Whereas ego says, "They make sandwiches; how hard is that?" "I'm too busy," or "I've earned this," EQ says, "How can I make the lives of my employees better now that I finally have the influence and resources to make it happen?"

The stark reality is that senior executives earn many multiples more than entry-level or average company employees. This wealth discrepancy is another factor that can make it easy for executives to lose touch with the real experience of frontline employees. I am reminded of the following story, told to me by one of my most valued employees, Lindsey, about her experience at a former employer.

It was a tough year at the property management company. Historically, the company gave out annual bonuses based on the company's performance, and by midyear rumors circulated that the year-end bonuses were at risk. Every few weeks, at her one-on-one meeting with her boss, Karen, the executive vice president of Human Resources, Lindsey would ask how the bonus situation was looking. Karen's usual response was, "I don't really know. Sorry." By early December, people were really starting to worry, and the lack of information about it had everyone on edge. So, again, Lindsey asked Karen about the bonus situation and mentioned that her staff was concerned about planning for holiday shopping and property taxes that were due that time of year. When Karen responded, she made a classic and memorable fall into Ego Trap 7. Karen rolled her eyes, and with a deep sigh said, "I am getting so sick of being asked about the bonuses! I still don't have any information to give you. Do they think I am not impacted by not getting a bonus? I have a brand-new, special-order BMW sitting on the lot that I cannot pick up until I get my bonus."

Wow! To her credit, Karen was genuinely trying to show some empathy that she was feeling the same pain that the rest of the employees were by not getting a bonus. Yet she succeeded only in proving without a shadow of a doubt that she had no real empathy at all. Instead of applying the EQ that the situation required, Karen's ego presented itself front and center. She didn't realize how far her own experience was from her employees, who weren't worried about luxury items, but looming year-end bills. Her credibility with Lindsey sank, as it did with the team who was informed that Karen could not provide any additional insight or clarification.

Could Karen, being an executive herself, have pressed her superiors for more information as year-end approached? Perhaps. And if not, she certainly could have tuned in better to what her workforce needed and communicated what little information she had with sensitivity to their financial needs. Calling a special meeting, sending a carefully worded e-mail, or giving Lindsey her humble apologies that she still did not have any information—any of these simple but effective means of communicating, "I hear you, I see you"—would have done wonders for her team's connection to her. Unfortunately, Karen had lost touch with the front-line workers because of the financial benefits of her own post. To her, no year-end bonus meant she'd have to forgo her coveted luxury car. She was clueless that for her people it meant they might not be able to buy their children holiday gifts or would have to dig into retirement savings in order to pay their property tax bills.

Ignore your people's needs, as Karen did, and they will find ways to ignore yours.

According to the Economic Policy Institute, CEOs made 231 times as much as their average employee in 2011.[13] To put that in perspective, if you are making $7 million a year as a CEO, your average employee is making along the lines of $30,000 per year, or $2,500 a month—*before* taxes and social security are taken out. Subtract rent, health insurance, grocery bills, and possibly child care, and there's not much, if anything, left to play with. Making hundreds of thousands or millions a year, as senior executives do, yields a whole different life experience.

Think of it this way. When you are making income on the scale of hundreds of thousands or millions of dollars, a $50 monthly hike in parking costs to move to the swanky new executive park or even a $10 cutback on the company-provided metro pass is not such a big deal. But when you're bringing home less than a thousand dollars every two weeks, that $50 hike or $10 cutback is painful. It can mean skipping the anniversary dinner out, not being able to pay for children's school supplies, or running up credit card debt to cover grocery bills. For the employee making average pay, that's demoralizing at best and deeply disturbing at worst.

Now, what was it about having a brand-new, special-order BMW just sitting on the lot that was stressing you out?

Periods of financial hardship for an organization, such as during pay freezes or layoffs, are a particularly important time for leaders to remain sensitive to the front line. The following story demonstrates why.

It began with an innocent e-mail sent by the CEO of a national home building company to his employees after he returned from an inspiring African safari in the Serengeti. It appears that the CEO, Roger, had hopes of using the e-mail to rally his troops to work hard through a difficult time, as the organization had recently been through at least two rounds of layoffs and needed to pull itself through the resultant pain. Unfortunately, a lack of sensitivity on Roger's part to the common experience of his frontline employees and some poorly worded musings landed him smack dab in the middle of Ego Trap 7.

Roger is purported to have stated in this e-mail, "Immersing oneself into the heart of the African bush is a soul-stirring experience." And, "For me, spending time in Africa put everything in perspective. I need to raise my game and take the initiative to identify key areas for personal improvement that will tangibly enhance my performance." Roger didn't do himself any favors as he waxed poetic about an exotic vacation that would be financially unobtainable to the majority of his organization's employees. What's more, in the stressful post-layoff period, when no employee feels his job is safe, luxury expenditures of any kind would be off the table. The result? Roger looked clueless and out of touch. But he didn't stop there. He is said to have continued with an analogy likening children to animals: "In the bush, young animals learn quickly that they are fully accountable for their own survival. In contrast, our kids are raised in a world of Little League Baseball and other sports where trophies are given out for mere participation."

There, don't you feel better?

Animal metaphor aside, Roger was essentially saying that people don't take enough accountability for their own situation in life. It may be a legitimate personal belief, but proclaiming it so publicly to employees who just witnessed coworkers, through no fault of their own, being laid off was Roger's giant, insensitive misstep into Ego Trap 7. It's a case of ego running the show with no empathy (EQ) on the premises.

When Roger's e-mail was leaked and publicized in the *Boston Herald*, comments from angry employees and the *Herald's* readership mushroomed online. Here are just a few reactions:

- "Read the 'inspiring' rich guy take on how the weak & old must die."
- "If he wants to live like a predatory animal, then he should go live WITH the predatory animals. Let's just see how he lives with that logic outside the immediate vicinity and safety of his Land Rover SUV."
- "Stop being an arrogant rich boy and lead with some sensitivity and understanding of what your employees face every day. Can you possibly be this tone deaf?"

Clearly, Roger raised the ire of regular individuals with his insensitivity. It is no surprise that the *Boston Herald* headline when the story broke showcased the words *chief* and *clueless* in the same line. When leaders fall into Ego Trap 7—falling out of touch with the front line— this is how they come across: self-absorbed, egotistical, and insensitive. Heightened situational awareness of the pain employees were going through, considering the post-layoff aftermath, could have tempered the kind of hubris and disconnectedness that Roger seemed to show with his e-mail.

Admittedly, it's easy to criticize Roger, especially in hindsight. Who among us hasn't sent at least one regrettable e-mail? But when you're a leader, the consequences of your actions, even seemingly small ones, take on a life of their own. How can you ensure you don't make a similar mistake? Only by putting EQ, rather than ego, in the driver's seat.

EQ Antidote: Recognizing, Reading, and Responding

As with any ego trap, the problem with Trap 7 is that you won't even know when you're stepping into it, unless you kick your EQ into high gear. Keeping the three Rs at the ready will help.

First, plan to regularly look within. Remember that your experience is very different from the average employee's, and *recognize* when your desires might not need to come first. Do you have the urge to send an e-mail waxing philosophic about your recent exotic vacation? Consider how that might come across to your average worker, remembering that others don't have the same financial cushion that you do. It's also important to get yourself out of the executive suite and onto the front line, sweating if you have to. If it makes you feel uncomfortable to step onto the factory floor or behind the sandwich counter, that's okay. Recognize and acknowledge your discomfort, consider the greater gain, and then throw yourself into it. It might even be fun.

At the end of the day, it's not about you anyway. It's about your organization and its people. It's about having empathy for your workforce. That's what a strong and effective leader does—looks out for the good of the people, within the context of growing a successful organization. By treating your employees well, you are helping to keep your employees engaged. And in the twenty-first century, we now know that engaged employees make for high-functioning and productive organizations.[14] It's a win-win for everyone. By making an effort to consciously *read* the temperature of the group, imagining how they feel in a specific moment based on their experiences, not yours, you will make better choices about what to say, what to do, and what decisions to make in any situation. You will lead in a way that feels connected to the group, respectful, and tuned in, not disconnected and clueless. This is what it looks like to be others-centric rather than self-centric.

Lastly, you can *respond*. With awareness of your own urges to make certain decisions or communicate certain things, and insight into how your workforce may be feeling at a given time, you will have the information you need to react and respond with self-control. If smartphones truly need to be eliminated to cut costs, you will be able to communicate this change with more sensitivity and have an informed game plan for minimizing business disruptions. Self-control gives you the discipline you need to shape your actions for the good of others; self-awareness and empathy give you the insight you need to make conscious decisions and to take sensitive actions. As a leader, your role is to bring the front line closer to you, not to allow yourself to drift—or push—too far away from it.

Stephanie, the executive vice president of HR at a real estate company where my team delivered some training, could have benefitted from an exercise using the three Rs. Partway through the training session, a frenzy broke out in the room as people noticed an e-mail on their smartphones notifying the group that layoffs were about to be announced. Chatter ensued and people thumbed through their phones with fear and nervousness. Above the din, as we got ready to break for lunch, Stephanie announced, "By the way, I can't stay for the afternoon session. I'm going golfing." Although she was actually trying to be helpful by communicating her upcoming absence, the effect and the timing were anything but helpful. I winced. Many in the group looked up at Stephanie, stunned. The sentiment was something like this: "People are about to lose their jobs, you're the head of HR, and you're going *golfing?*" Insensitive and out of touch doesn't even begin to describe the negative thoughts about Stephanie that were swirling through the room. It was a blundering step into Ego Trap 7.

How might this situation have played out differently if she had demonstrated some EQ? First, Stephanie could have exercised some self-awareness, remembering that "I am in a privileged position here to be able to go golfing, to know I'm not getting laid off, and to have influence over many of the people in this room." Second, Stephanie could have exercised some empathy, keeping an attitude that says, "I can only imagine how everyone in the room is feeling right now, hearing that their jobs are in jeopardy. I am sure it's anything from angry and threatened to stressed and worried. This can't be easy news to hear." Third, Stephanie could have blended self-awareness, empathy, and self-control into a useful response, communicating, "I'm in a unique position as a leader to put the group at ease. What actions can I take or statements can I make to be the leader that the group needs me to be?" If Stephanie had worked her way through each of the three Rs, she would likely have chosen a different approach than to announce her golfing plans to the group. The choices at her disposal? Cancel golf or quietly slip away, and then check in at the end of the day. And that's the very low-hanging fruit.

At a minimum, communicating her golfing plans with extreme sensitivity would have been helpful. Instead, her broad public announcement came across as if it were just another day at the office. Out of touch with the frontline workers? Stephanie wasn't even on the same planet. She was roundly mocked as word got out about her golf outing, and the day left a bad taste in the mouths of both the employees who were eventually laid off and, worse, the ones who stayed. About a year later, after a series of similar gaffes, Stephanie was demoted.

GE gives us a wonderful example of not only how to stay in touch with frontline workers but how to leverage their insight to the company's benefit. It all started in the mid-1990s under the leadership of the renowned Jack Welch when the company rolled out their "workout" sessions. In a series of town-hall-style meetings that involved more than 200,000 GE employees, the executives investigated what frontline individuals believed were barriers to successful operations and what customer needs weren't being met. A lot of people have suggested that these local gatherings, which brought people into groups of thirty to one hundred to discuss problems, were what led to GE's astounding success in the following decade. Since that time, many other organizations have emulated these meetings with frontline workers, modeling GE's success.

What I've learned from workers I've interviewed while coaching their bosses is that the interaction doesn't always have to be as formal as the workout session or town hall. Just having the leader show up at the company picnic or attend a birthday party on the factory floor goes a long way for people. Why? When the executive is chatting with people one on one, these individuals will talk and share important information, whether about operational challenges, an idea for a new initiative, or feedback on how the new equipment is working. Leaders get amazing insight into the company, their employees, and their challenges simply by showing up and talking to their people. It is a way for the leader to say to the group, "You're more important to me right now than the board of directors and all those people waiting for me. I'm going to be with you instead." That little bit of attention ultimately builds morale, increases engagement, and augments loyalty. Most frontline workers know that the CEO is busy and they truly appreciate any time spent with them.

In a Nutshell

How aware are you of what matters to the front line? Is your "open door" policy something you say, or do people really take you up on it? Even the best senior executives can find themselves sealed off from the company's day-to-day realities, whether it's because employees need an appointment or a badge to visit the executive suite, a receptionist defensively manages the calendar, or the exec's door really is always closed, literally or figuratively.

Ego Trap 7 is ready and waiting to lure you in because it's easy to lose touch when you are removed from the front line, occupied with board meetings, visiting with customers, and speaking at association conferences. Leaders—including those executives in the national and international spotlight—fall into this trap all the time. Consider, for example, the Detroit automobile executives who flew to Washington D.C. in their private jets to ask Congress for funds to avoid bankruptcy. It's no surprise that Congress blasted them. Next time around? The executives drove their cars. And we can't forget British Petroleum's Tony Hayward, who had the gumption to sail his yacht off the Isle of Wight "as the tar balls washed up on the Gulf Coast" during the world's worst petroleum spill, who in the middle of it all, delivered that crisis-PR sound bite from hell: "I'd like my life back."[15] As Gulf fishermen wondered how they'd feed their families and Florida hoteliers were faced with closing their doors, Hayward announced to the world he was ready to resume his life of power and privilege. How nice it would be if the fishermen and tourism workers could do the same. It was a luxury unavailable to these folks on the front line.

Can *we* have your life back, Tony?

How will you stay connected to your workers' daily experience? It's not about pandering or over-catering. It's about connecting in a way that keeps you informed so you have a read on where you can make effective changes and how to deliver them, where you should reconsider, and where you should hold your ground. Like a chess game in which you become able to look into the future, staying connected to your front line helps you envision consequences before your next move so you can elicit what you hope for and avoid unintended outcomes. It also has the potential to provide you with fresh ideas and perspectives—key information about your products and services--that can help you move through problems, open up growth, and envision new possibilities. Those on the ground often have a keen understanding of their operations and of what the customer really needs. And there's no substitute for that perspective.

Do you have to visit the front line regularly? Truth be told, many of your workers won't expect it. If leaders don't make appearances, people aren't surprised and the leader may not even take a huge credibility hit. But when leaders do make the gesture of spending time with their people, or when they make insightful decisions that are sensitive to the front line, they get a bazillion bonus credibility points. The result is an engaged and loyal workforce. Priceless.

APPLYING THE THREE R'S

Recognize that you may be out of touch with the front line of your organization or that you may seem out of reach to them (self-awareness). While some distance is natural, and sometimes unavoidable, recognizing it is the first step toward bridging the gap.

Read what frontline employees really need through their spoken and unspoken cues (empathy). Frontline workers may not provide outright feedback, but if you ask them questions that reflect sincere interest, you can establish a connection and encourage them to share their invaluable perspective with you. These grateful employees are more than likely to pass on word of this positive experience, and many other similarly rewarding moments will follow.

Respond with appreciation for the efforts of your frontline workers and be as specific as possible. Even when the feedback they offer is difficult to hear, exercise self-control and keep your focus on their needs. When the stakes are high and employees dare to share with you, they deserve respect and appreciation. When you make others feel seen, heard, and valued you will unleash performance in them like you never thought possible.

Ego Trap 8

Relapsing Back to Your Old Ways

Unfortunately, there is only one "sin" greater than falling into any of the Ego Traps described so far in this book—and that is making positive changes to your behavior, avoiding a trap, and then falling back into old behaviors again. It's called an ego relapse—the damaging descent from newfound emotional intelligence right back into whatever ego pitfall has traditionally been your weak spot. Unfortunately, as we will discuss in a moment, this relapse creates more damage than failing to avoid the trap in the first place.

Enter Ego Trap 8, which happens when leaders go back to their old, low-EQ ways and ruin their credibility among the team in the process. Here are a few examples:

- Isabela, who was long disliked by her team because of the last-minute work demands she'd place on them on Friday afternoons (Ego Trap 5—being blind to downstream impact), began to delegate work earlier in the week after receiving 360-degree feedback that her last-minute approach was problematic for her team. Six months later, however, when her organization did not pass inspection by a national certifying agency, Isabela resumed overloading employees with work on Friday afternoons to ensure that they stopped "slacking off."

- Cliff was known for not letting go of operational control but finally started delegating and letting his team take some risks after realizing his blind spot was stymieing his company's growth. A year after this change, one of his employees made a bad decision, which sent Cliff into a relapse. He overreacted by once again getting involved in every decision.

- After working with a coach, Don discovered that he was known for crushing opposing viewpoints during meetings. In response, he began making a conscious effort to listen and ask questions when someone raised perspectives counter to his own. Unfortunately, when Don suffered a back injury, his irritability ratcheted up and his patience dwindled. The result? He resumed steamrolling team members who did not immediately go along with his viewpoint during conversations and meetings.

Ego Trap 8 is triggered when leaders shift from high-ego to high-EQ behavior—demonstrating the *potential* to be self-aware, empathic, and self-disciplined—only to slip back into the same high-ego behaviors they exhibited in the past. Others see that the leader is capable of change when she is focused and motivated to do so. And she proves herself capable of acting sensitively and using self-control and situational awareness. Until she doesn't. This sends a message to others that these leaders are *choosing* to act with low EQ. This in turn leads to a credibility breach so deep that team members no longer trust and believe in these leaders. If perception and loyalty were on the line before changing, there are even more important things at stake when it comes to sustaining it.

According to Merriam-Webster's online dictionary, *credibility* is "the quality or power of inspiring belief."[1] Wikipedia describes *credibility* as "believability of a source or message," including "trustworthiness."[2] Within the leadership realm, I see *credibility* as the bank of trust leaders build up between themselves and their teams, which gives the followers confidence in their leaders' reliability, dependability, and authenticity. With credibility, leaders demonstrate "the integrity, intent, capabilities, and results" that make them believable to themselves and others.[3] Without credibility, however, teams lose respect for their leaders' authority and question leaders' ability to do the job. What's more, individuals' motivation to give their best to their leaders wanes.

Not that I am suggesting it, but if you show low EQ across the board, your team may not like you, but they will probably forgive you, saying things like, "He can't help himself" or "She doesn't know any better." In contrast, if you are known for having low EQ, but make positive changes, demonstrating you are *capable* of high EQ, and then revert to bad behaviors, your team won't just *not* forgive you. They'll start to despise you. "He can't help himself" is replaced with "I've seen him act more sensitively, and right now he is choosing to be a jerk." "She doesn't know any better" becomes "She knows exactly what she's doing when she acts that way, but she doesn't respect us enough to do anything about it." From your team's point of view it's a case of "Where'd our new boss go?"

Is this fair to leaders? Maybe, maybe not. We all have bad days and spells where we get tired of applying more effort. This is perhaps even more true in the realm of EQ, because real change can be so uncomfortable at times and it takes a good deal of energy and attention to maintain new behaviors. But, there seems to be a very real backlash by employees against leaders who are inconsistent in displaying their EQ skills. Now, before any of you get the smart idea to throw this whole EQ thing in the trash, thinking maybe it's better not to do anything at all than to risk the huge fallout of a relapse ("If they've tolerated me this long maybe it's best to leave well enough alone and not set myself up to fail in the eyes of my followers"), stop right here and ask yourself why you and your company don't deserve more. The payoff of having EQ will always out-value the investment required to use and *keep using* it.

A Closer Look at the Trap

To see Ego Trap 8 in action, we can return to the story of Gary, the executive and legal genius who often treated his direct reports poorly, believing that his technical prowess as an attorney excused him from applying sensitivity, empathy, or any other aspect of EQ in his team interactions. For example, Gary used a combative tone with his team, made them feel stupid for asking questions, and turned every discussion into a debate.

Yet, as Gary and I worked together, a kinder, more tuned-in leader emerged. Gary learned to recognize when his argumentative nature was getting in the way of communicating with his team (self-awareness). He learned how to tone it down and read situations for unspoken cues that could help him connect with his people (empathy), including when to play "attorney" Gary and when to play "leader" Gary. He began to respond in ways that were less rigid and abrasive, opting for more flexibility and fluidity (self-control). Six months later, after a lot of intense work on his part, Gary had amazed everyone with his progress—even himself. He had boosted his EQ in big ways that had changed his management dynamic for the better and built up his credibility with his entire team. I hoped that Gary's story would have a happy ending.

Unfortunately, Ego Trap 8 kicked in. In Gary's case, thirty days after the coaching engagement ended, I followed up with him and he told me he felt he was doing well. By my 120-day phone call to him, he admitted that a few bad old behaviors had started to crop up, but he promised he was addressing the issues. Nine months later, after I checked in with his Human Resources VP, I learned that Gary had sunk back into most of his old, problematic interactions with others. Now people were less forgiving: if earlier they had given him a pass, assuming he didn't know any better, this time they had seen Gary change and knew he was capable of better. Now they knew he *could* do it but was *choosing* not to. His credibility took such a hit that, at the one-year anniversary of the end of our coaching engagement, the firm demoted him. With the drop in responsibility and status came a substantial pay cut. This was not the ending most leaders desire, that's for sure.

Take note: this trap can have serious consequences.

What happened to Gary? What triggered Ego Trap 8 for him? In his case, I believe that his desire and motivation to be an effective leader wasn't great enough to sustain the focus and hard work it required to exercise daily EQ-centric behavior. It didn't come naturally or easily to him, and over time he just let it slip. Instead of remaining vigilant, he resorted to what felt comfortable: his old, high-ego ways. Instead of continuing to practice what he learned during our work together, he got complacent, perhaps telling himself that he had changed enough and proven what he needed to. He may also have mistakenly perceived these gains as permanent, even though his outside behaviors were clearly slipping back into place and people stopped providing him with feedback. In addition, he missed seeing this silence as a sign that individuals were once again uncomfortable being honest with him.

It's not that Gary was a bad person; it's just that his tendency for high-ego behavior required sustained effort to overcome. He had to want to be an effective leader strongly enough that he would keep working the program he and I had laid down together, even when he got tired, the job got stressful, or challenging situations arose.

This dynamic is much like the challenges of physical fitness. Going to the gym, working out with a friend, or exercising at home are great methods for creating positive change, but none of them is permanent. Health, fitness, and weight loss must be cultivated and maintained over time. It isn't a project; it's a lifelong priority. Once you've lost the weight, you have to continue exercising regularly and maintaining your diet, or you'll gain it all back and risk even greater health issues.

Similarly, Gary had to continue to exercise self-awareness, empathy, and self-control each and every day at the office, or he would risk reverting to the "insensitive jerk" that his direct reports had once decried. Sadly, Gary stopped practicing the three Rs of EQ (recognizing, reading, and responding) and turned back into a pumpkin—a rotten one at that, which his team could no longer excuse.

Leaders fall into Ego Trap 8 for a variety of reasons, including stress, distraction, complacency, discomfort with practicing EQ, or any other issue that causes the leader to take his eye off the EQ "ball." It doesn't help that others are hesitant to give honest feedback to leaders, given the power and status associated with those at the top. For example, Gary's direct reports were unlikely to tell him, "Hey, boss, you're treating us really badly right now." Yet, they didn't hesitate to complain about him behind his back and to his superiors.

Think of it this way. At a gut level, employees who see a leader use EQ in one moment but descend into using ego the next may feel betrayed. "He can make this easier on us, but once again, it's all about him" is one common criticism. Just as bad are comments like, "I knew she wouldn't be able to stick with it" and "We all knew Mr. Nice Guy was never going to last."

It's not just a matter of disrespecting the leader; it's a matter of broken credibility. Adjusting from high-ego to high-EQ behavior then falling back to high-ego behavior tells your team that you are unpredictable, can't be trusted, and, frankly, are too weak to make positive change. *Gulp.* It starts to become clear why Ego Trap 8 can be so damaging to the leader's reputation. Your team stuck with you during your transformation, before which you jerked them around on a daily emotional roller coaster. Now you're sending signals that they need to go through that again? Why would they do that to themselves? You have essentially used up all the emotional capital you've earned. Your team will have a short tolerance for it, and they will start looking for a stronger leader to follow.

The EQ Faucet: Is It On or Off?

Is it really any surprise that acting mercurially, with high EQ one day and with low EQ another, raises the ire and breaks the trust of your people? This kind of behavior often leads to perceptions of an individual as "duplicitous," "slippery," "political, or "fake." These are not characteristics that anyone wants in an executive leader. The following story of superstar salesman—but awful boss—Cameron tells the tale in high definition.

As general manager and senior vice president at a mail order company, Cameron had both inward- and outward-facing responsibilities. On the one hand, he spent his time in the field interfacing with potential and current customers to generate additional business for his division of the company; on the other hand, at his home office he managed a dozen employees who were responsible for processing orders. Cameron was utterly at ease with the sales part of his job, resulting in his division outperforming the revenue of every other division of the company by a two-to-one ratio. Yet Cameron's entire office staff had turned over *four times* in three years. Something was definitely wrong. Because Cameron was clearly a high-value employee to his organization, the division president hired me to help Cameron make some adjustments to reduce the disruption and associated costs of his massive office turnover.

After spending a morning with Cameron in the field visiting customers, I was blown away by the high EQ he demonstrated. "I have nothing to teach him," I thought to myself as I watched Cameron read every individual in the room. He knew who to approach and who not to bother. He remembered the names of people's pets and children. And when Cameron gave a presentation to a buying group, he was careful to talk right at everyone's level—not up or down—avoiding using jargon and industry lingo. Cameron clearly had control over his behavior and an ability to filter it through an empathic lens.

Imagine my surprise when later that afternoon Cameron and I returned to his office and he shifted from speaking with sensitivity, self-awareness, and empathy to speaking abruptly and rudely to his office staff. "Get me this." "Don't do that." "I don't want to catch you on a personal phone call again." "I don't care if you have to work late, just get it done." You name it, if it was insensitive, Cameron said it, loud and proud. I watched in disbelief—who was this person? Cameron seemed like a totally different individual from the considerate, attuned man I had witnessed in front of customers earlier in the day. My new client was Dr. Jekyll and Mr. Hyde.

What was going on here? Cameron was an example of someone who turns the EQ on and off. The reality is that, even if someone has a high EQ, he has the free will to use it or not. I sometimes see it in the workplace: people turn the EQ on for the boss but off for their staff, on for their customers but off for their peers. On at the office, off for their spouse. This is another version of Ego Trap 8—when leaders apply their EQ in some situations but not others. This chameleonlike behavior and manipulation of EQ can get leaders into trouble.

Cameron's problems began the moment his employees saw him treating his clients with sensitivity and consideration, a sharp contrast to the way he usually treated his own staff. Customers would sometimes come to his office to sign paperwork, at which point Cameron would turn on his EQ charm. Seconds after a customer departed, Cameron turned his EQ off and went back to treating his staff with insensitivity and arrogance. Naturally, his team saw the stark difference in the way Cameron treated customers versus the way he treated them, and it enraged them. Cameron was *capable* of listening, adjusting, and putting the needs of others before his own, but only if he saw them as valuable enough to do so. As for his home team? He seemed to deem them unworthy by not bothering to extend the same courtesies to them. This wasn't just disrespectful, it was dehumanizing. Cameron's employees, unhappy in a miserable work environment with a seemingly inauthentic, insensitive boss who knew better, routinely became disenchanted and quit.

Although it can be tempting, it's not okay to use your EQ with people whom you think are worth it while giving yourself an EQ pass with people you deem less important. It's not just about fairness; it's that inconsistently applying your EQ skills can hurt you as a leader. When others see you turn your EQ on and off like a faucet—and not extend it to them—they may no longer want to work for you, which can lead to the kinds of steep turnover that Cameron saw, resulting in higher costs, inefficiency, and disrupted work flow.

In addition, turning the EQ faucet on and off may also alienate your peers as they begin to develop a view of you as slick and superficial—or as they suffer from your mistreatment of them. Yet your peers are essential to your success over the long term at any organization. They are your stakeholders, and when you are not in the room, they are the ones who have the potential to advocate for you *or against you*. My experience, after seeing different scenarios play out, is that not having a fan club is usually career limiting. It is these key relationships, as much as those with your direct reports, that must not be neglected when it comes to using your EQ. Wise executives understand that relationships with support staff like IT, accounting, and HR are vital. Even though they may seem peripheral, EQ says that each person in your network is as essential as the others.

YOU KNOW YOU'VE FALLEN INTO EGO TRAP 8 IF . . .

- You find yourself operating on autopilot, not making mindful choices in interactions with others.
- You think you have "fixed things" and don't need to worry about having EQ goals anymore. You see these changes as tasks to be checked off your list rather than as an attitude to be exercised over the long term.
- You see certain audiences as worthy of your best efforts while others, in your view, are not.
- On good days you demonstrate high EQ but feel justified in letting it slide on bad days. Having high EQ doesn't mean I have to be perfect, right?

The Battle of Ego vs. EQ

It's a matter of what wins out—the ego or emotional intelligence. Ego encourages going to that place of doing what comes comfortably and reflexively. So whichever trap you struggle most to avoid, ego will tell you it's okay to retreat there from time to time. Hey, you're the leader and you've got a lot on your plate. So what if you get a little lazy and ignore some recent feedback from a team member (Ego Trap 1), fill just one job opening with someone who acts and thinks a lot like you do (Ego Trap 3), or level jump and give work to someone a few rungs down the chain of command just because you know that person will get it done (Ego Trap 5)? You should be able let your EQ down from time to time, right?

Maybe, but then again, maybe not. It's a slippery slope. Just like one day missed at the gym can turn into a week, and then a month, so too can a self-granted hiatus from EQ become an indefinite vacation that lands you at the bottom of Ego Trap 8—the insufferable leader who knows better but chooses not to make the effort. (Paging Dr. Jekyll . . .)

In Cameron's case, once we worked together to raise his self-awareness of his tendency to turn his emotional intelligence on and off, he was better able to leverage the EQ skills he already had with his staff and make significant improvement on his overall effectiveness, including his turnover rate. When EQ rules the roost, diligence and a dash of humility reign. You know that it's hard work to consistently apply self-awareness, empathy, and self-control, and you don't give yourself a free pass to skip it because you recognize that consistency is what counts. You realize that you have to follow through on your new high-EQ approach to remain a credible leader, or else people won't believe you've really changed.

Is it okay to make mistakes from time to time? Actually, it is. It helps people see you as relatable. What matters more is how you handle it and recover. Will you always be the paragon of high EQ? Probably not. I have been immersed in this subject matter for decades now and still find myself drifting off course. We all have our challenging moments, and we are all human. Keep in mind, too, that by keeping that trust account you have with your team high, you can afford to make a few withdrawals. So you don't have to be perfect or an EQ superhero. The goal instead is to maintain a *sincere desire over the long term* to keep your EQ toned and to stay in connection with those people and tools that help keep you accountable and growing. Where there is intention to maintain high EQ, behavior can follow. But when intention dwindles, ego sees an open door to sneak back in and jump behind the steering wheel, conspiratorially whispering in your ear, "You're tired, let me drive."

The lessons offered in this book do not represent some magic program that can be implemented for a month and then put to rest after a tidy graduation. Instead, each chapter offers guideposts that need to be visited time and again to gauge how you are doing, to measure your progress, and to ensure sustained commitment and attention. Putting a system of regular feedback in place, such as the 360-degree assessment and/or working with a qualified coach on an ongoing basis can help to keep your attention to EQ sharp. Surrounding yourself with others who have high EQ can also help as you lift one another up on a difficult day (of all the tools I use to keep my EQ robust, this is my personal favorite).

To better understand how ego versus EQ plays a role here, let's look at the difference between Gary and another client of mine named Rick, who managed to avoid Trap 8. First, a little about Rick. As vice president at a large technology company, Rick maintained an excellent relationship with the division president. His relationships with his team, however, were not as strong. Rick, who held his team to high standards, didn't know it, but he intimidated the people he managed. As it turns out, his team members performed to Rick's standards not out of any positive motivation but out of fear of looking stupid in front of him or to avoid getting fired. Yet Rick was oblivious to his reputation. A master's degree program in organizational behavior at the prestigious Case Western Reserve University provided Rick with a sudden wake-up call. Working through the program, Rick participated in 360-degree assessments that revealed, to his chagrin, his actual reputation around the company.

In response, Rick embarked on a journey to increase his EQ in the workplace, beginning by mindfully connecting to his employees on things that mattered to *them* instead of *him*. He managed his impulse to demand work and started collaborating more, asking for input on deadlines and project scopes—inspiring high standards of performance and earning his team's total respect in the process. It wasn't long after this transformation occurred that the then-division president was promoted to CEO and moved Rick into the role of division president. It was at this moment that it would have been easy for Rick to fall into Ego Trap 8. He now had even more power—a strong potential ego trigger—as well as additional responsibility and stress in his job, which all could have taken his focus off of his EQ effort or may have helped him rationalize a relapse. He also could have grown complacent, telling himself, "Now that I'm really top dog, I can do as I please."

With his ego in check and his EQ in the lead, Rick understood that it was at exactly this point that he couldn't let up. First, he did not want to undermine the strides he'd made to date. Second, he recognized that he was a far more effective leader with his EQ at the ready, and, surprisingly, he was happier too. He would need EQ to help him navigate the new challenges he faced as division president, so he continued his own development work. Partnering with me as his coach, he focused on honing the EQ trinity—his self-awareness, empathy, and self-control—even more. Reading the environment and the people in it is always a moving target, requiring nimble situational readiness. And the reality was that the landscape was completely different now. Rick had new direct reports, new stakeholders, and a whole new slew of peers. Working diligently on his EQ goals, Rick garnered tremendous admiration and loyalty from his team. And, following his lead, the next two levels of leaders have made personal development a priority. Twenty-four months after Rick's promotion, the organization is experiencing record growth and market share.

Now let's compare Rick's story with Gary's. Although it's always difficult to identify exactly which factors combine to cause a person's behavior, I would venture to guess that Gary found it so uncomfortable and difficult to apply his EQ that he consciously or unconsciously allowed himself to return to his old ways. At first it was probably a little here and there; then he let go full steam as he slipped deeper and deeper into his ego relapse. Every individual must decide whether the effort of applying EQ is worth it; whatever the decision, there will be consequences, either negative or positive. EQ brings great power but we must choose to use it, and to use it for good.

Whereas ego says, "Bask in the positive feedback, look how far I've come," EQ remembers, "This is hard work and I can't ever let up." Whereas ego says, "I'm justified to act this way because of circumstances," EQ says, "I know better and can only behave in a manner I would desire from others." While ego questions, "Why can't they just accept me as I am?" EQ asks, "What do I really gain by going backward?"

When it comes to leading with EQ, follow-through is critical to success. By thinking of EQ as a muscle you need to exercise regularly to keep it strong—as opposed to thinking of it as a tool you acquire through a one-time investment—you can keep an attitude of commitment and focus that will hold you in good stead even with the occasional challenges that will come your way and tempt ego slipups.

EQ Antidote: Recognizing, Reading, and Responding

To avoid slipping back into high-ego behavior—whether by losing touch with the front line, surrounding yourself with more of you, being blind to your downstream impact, or any of the other ego traps—you can draw on your trusty EQ tools of recognizing, reading, and responding.

Self-awareness—or *recognizing* what's happening with you—will go a long way to help you avoid a full relapse into your old ways. The trick is to catch yourself before you slide too far back into old and comfortable ego territory. You can do that by checking in with yourself from time to time and asking the right questions. How are you acting in a given moment and how are you interacting? If your common ego trap is to hold tight to control, check in from time to time and ask yourself how well you are doing with delegating to others and allowing them to see a task through. If your common ego trap is thinking that your technical expertise gives you permission to treat others condescendingly, have you been able of late to pause and be a better listener? Or have you been cutting yourself too much ego slack lately, rationalizing impatience and allowing yourself to interrupt others so you can give the answer?

Ask others how you are doing to help you get a more realistic picture. Accountability partners are a must because if your self-awareness is low, self-questioning can produce the wrong answers. Being honest about your own growth challenges takes courage; that willingness to be real and to work hard, out in the open, won't go unnoticed by your team. They will see that courage as a sort of fearlessness, a sign of strength.

When keeping your EQ "monitor" active, take time to look outward too. Be sure to give consistent energy to *reading* what's going on with the people around you (empathy). If you noticed positive reactions when you started applying high-EQ behavior, ask yourself whether those positive reactions have been sustained or if people have gone back to grumbling under their breath, squeaking out minor complaints, or avoiding you. If you get a different reaction from people than when you first started turning on the EQ, then you are probably behaving differently too! (Note: People often try to hide their disdain from the leader, so their responses to you may not always be hyper-evident, but try to tune in to the subtle clues, such as "friendly reminders," critiques masked as jokes, feedback sent via someone they know you will listen to, or deafening silence.)

Remember to put yourself in other people's shoes and try to imagine how you would feel under their circumstances. If you've just implemented a new policy, how would you feel about it if you were working on the assembly line or in the field with customers? When you assign a task to your staff, think about what it will take for them to get it done at their level, not yours. And if you feel tempted to close up the bar at the holiday party, pause to ask yourself how this might appear to your people (or on YouTube). By regularly asking yourself the questions, "How might others perceive me?" and "How would I feel in that person's position?" you can keep your empathy muscle strong.

While self-awareness and empathy give you the data you need to avoid Ego Trap 8, it's the *responding* piece of the puzzle that will ultimately help you sidestep the kind of damaging reactions and behaviors that can trigger Trap 8. After recognizing when you're feeling stressed, for example, you can use self-control to avoid the kind of high-ego responses that are tempting under such circumstances. After considering other people's perspectives, you can adjust accordingly when selecting a strategy. Self-awareness and self-control always work well together, helping you notice when you have gone out of bounds behaving from a place of ego instead. You can acknowledge it to the group, ask for forgiveness, and correct your course.

When you *recognize* the ego traps you fall into most often, you can renew your relationship with the whole company—bolstering your effectiveness at all levels. When you remember to *read* situations and people in order to know when to use your array of EQ skills, you will shake any poor perceptions that had been part of your "story" and replace them with evidence of your competence and effectiveness as a leader.

Responding whenever possible to the daily challenges of your business with appropriate measures of self-awareness, empathy, and self-control builds the kind of credibility that can reengage your workforce and energize the entire organization around your vision.

In a Nutshell

It is natural over time to drift into your comfort zone, whatever that may be. For some of you, that means getting involved in operations when you should stay on a higher level. For others, it's hiring people that look and think like you do. And for others it's using your technical expertise too aggressively, hogging the opportunities to shine. Even if you make strides over time to mitigate these tendencies, stress, fatigue, distraction, and other factors can emerge and pull you off course for a time. The situation becomes more complex when you consider that you are not likely to get a lot of feedback and input from others on your performance, as no one wants to put his neck out by calling out the chief executive on bad behavior.

While your odds of success are high, be aware that employees are often unforgiving of those leaders who show they are capable of acting with high EQ and then go back to their former high-ego ways. Cameron, the master salesman from the mail order company who lost his entire office staff four times, ended up outlasting six peers when a severe industry downturn resulted in the closing of the company's offices. The president confirmed to me that it was not only his sales expertise but also his sustained EQ that saved him. On the other hand, Gary's direct reports skewered him for his ego relapse and he ended up with a demotion.

As a successful executive you know that results don't happen on their own. You know that anything worth having is worth working for, and EQ is no different. Most executives and entrepreneurs I know have not chosen the easy path. They are the fearless, driven type of leaders who don't run from a challenge and are willing to take on the toughest task of all—changing themselves.

I once gave a keynote on how important it is for leaders to work on strengthening their EQ and mentioned this idea that it's okay to share when you are struggling. One audience member raised his hand and said, "That's ridiculous. If a leader is struggling and admits it, he will look weak and no one will respect him." Yet another audience member disagreed, saying, "When leaders share that they are struggling, I like them more. It tells me that it's okay to not be perfect and that the leader is human." Perfectly put, I'd say.

APPLYING THE THREE RS

Recognize that you will naturally drift back to ego, especially in times of challenge, fatigue, or stress. Use your self-awareness to tune in to your moods, emotions, and impulses from time to time. Do you have a handle on them, keeping them in balance with empathy and self-control? Or have you started slipping back into high-ego ways? Consider assigning someone you trust to look for any signs of relapse, and give this person permission to call you on it right away.

Read what those around you are trying to communicate to you. Are others giving you subtle clues that you have relapsed into old ego behaviors by making masked jokes, or retreating into radio silence? Before you let yourself slip too far back into old ego behaviors, remember that others may see you as weak, untrustworthy, or not genuine if you regress and return to your previous ways. Identify someone you feel demonstrates very high EQ and use that person to check your accuracy. After interactions and group meetings the person also attended, set some time with this observer to share what you noticed, what it told you, and how you can use it to benefit yourself and others. Validating areas you nailed, and learning what you may have missed or misread, puts you in a constant state of growth.

Respond by renewing your intention to act with EQ, because success comes from commitment. When you're having a bad day, be honest about that with others and acknowledge the negative impact it likely had on them. When you're honest, sincere, and committed to working on your EQ on good days and bad, people will accept you for being human.

Conclusion

When it comes to the ego traps, the journey is a personal one, unique to each of us. We will all struggle in different ways and have our own tendencies to regularly fall into some traps while managing to avoid others easily. The individuals you've met in this book certainly show us how these traps may affect us and those important to us, as well as the risks and rewards associated with the way we decide to manage ego temptations. Recall Henri, the dapper Frenchman who lost his cool when given feedback from his team ("Am I really that way? Give me an example!") and fell into Ego Trap 1 (ignoring feedback you don't like). Then there was Jeanine, the successful shoe store owner who hired her look-alike for the position of general manager, someone who excelled in sales but really needed to be strong in inventory and personnel management (Ego Trap 3—surrounding yourself with more of you). Remember Marty, the fiery business founder who struggled to keep his hands out of operations (Trap 4—not letting go of control) and his foot out of his mouth (Trap 6—underestimating how much you're being watched). And there was business owner Meredith, who hijacked an entire day from her director of HR in order to complete her own to-do list when she came back into town from a shortened vacation (Trap 5—being blind to your downstream impact). We cannot forget Karen, the HR EVP at the property management company who impatiently rebuffed repeated inquiries about the status of holiday bonuses by sharing her own anxiety about whether she would be able to pick up her "special-order BMW" (Trap 7—losing touch with the front line). And Gary, the legal genius who felt his technical expertise excused him from treating people civilly (Trap 2—believing your technical skills trump your leadership skills). Gary then fixed his ways, only to revert nine months later to his high-ego behavior (Trap 8—relapsing back to your old ways)

All of these individuals suffered the consequences of their particular ego traps. For example:

- Jeanine cost her business roughly 10 percent in revenue due to poor administration of inventory as well as an increase in employee turnover.
- Marty's effectiveness as a leader was compromised, with his performance being rated by his team as only a six on a scale of one to ten.
- After sinking back into most of his old, problematic interactions with others, Gary got demoted and was handed a pay cut.

Whether it is employee disengagement, lowered morale, increased turnover, or decreased motivation, the effects of falling into the ego traps are real and costly. At best, leaders who chronically fall into the ego traps irritate their people, eat away at their own credibility, and make life difficult for followers. At worst, they may sabotage their odds of success and whittle down the performance potential of their people. Corporate scandals and PR issues are also common symptoms of ego run amuck, whether because of the kind of poor judgment that says skinny-dipping at a company event is okay (Ego Trap 6) or because a tendency to hire look-alikes has resulted in a team that doesn't challenge corporate practices, leading to the release of products harmful to consumers (Ego Trap 3).

No one ever said executive leadership would be easy. The nature of executives' work actually *sets them up* to fall into one or more of the eight ego traps, whether because of the burden of power that comes with the executive territory or the natural push and pull dynamics between leader and followers.

Perhaps it's the fact that there are few individuals above you to provide complete honesty compared with the hoards below whose primary desire is to please those above them. Or perhaps it's that you have so much power it's easy to stop worrying about what other people think. Either way, there will often be a sort of power bubble around you, which makes it easy to slip into "ego mode" and lose touch with the way others view you. This is not a matter of being good or bad—it just seems to be inherent in the position.

The higher you go, the more likely you are to face the need to up your professional game to meet ever stiffer leadership challenges along the way. Frankly, if the climb were easy, everyone would take a shot at the C-Suite or at starting her own business. But, the herd naturally thins as the terrain becomes tougher to navigate: the ego traps are doing their evolutionary work.

The Time and Attention Factor

You may have heard the old expression that it takes twenty-one days to create a new habit, effectively retraining your body and mind to make new behaviors stick. Exercising EQ is no exception, so give yourself a few weeks of using your EQ in a conscious way before you look for it to come more instinctively. If it feels awkward or time-consuming at first, don't quit. That's a perfectly normal reaction, so stick with your program and just remember that in a short time it will become second nature.

As leading neuroscientist David Rock has shown us, attention and focus also play an important role when it comes to making permanent behavior change. As Rock and his coauthor, Jeffrey Schwartz, describe in the following passage from their article "The Neuroscience of Leadership," scientists:

> now...know that the brain changes as a function of where an individual puts his or her attention. The power is in the focus... Among the implications: People who practice a specialty every day literally think differently, through different sets of connections, than do people who don't practice the specialty.[1]

If you are able to put an intentional focus on exercising your EQ with consistent, mindful effort, the wiring in your brain will start to change too, so that you respond using emotional intelligence more reflexively and with greater ease. As your environment starts to respond to your positive changes with its own positive responses, the cycle of high-EQ behavior is reinforced. When you see the desirable results of your hard work, it will motivate you, pulling you closer to your desired outcomes and better business results with less and less conscious effort.

Do you have to be focused on sharpening your EQ twenty-four hours a day? Fortunately, Rock has shown us that the answer to that question is no. Instead, the best way to develop new behaviors comes in minutes of attention a day versus hours a week.[2] That's good news for busy executives.

Once you've identified your common ego trap(s), you can start by setting an intention to work on avoiding them in bursts throughout the day—for example, when you first enter the office, at lunch, and at the afternoon staff meeting or on your morning or evening commute. Whether it's for five minutes before you leave the office or on your ride home from work, you can do a quick recap of how you interacted with others that day and assess your progress, considering what you could have done better or differently. The goal is to continually train your mind to exercise self-awareness, empathy, and self-control a few times or minutes a day and then watch the benefits unfold as your emotional intelligence starts to flow more naturally through all of your interactions. (See the Ego Trap 8 chapter for additional tips on maintaining EQ over time.) Interestingly, you will also begin to see these areas more noticeably in others too. These can be excellent visual reminders of what not to do as we see others step in ego quicksand. It can also provide you with positive reinforcement when you begin to discover everyday EQ role models all around you.

What's Your Story?

The good news is that none of us will fall into all of the ego traps; usually, we have just one or two that tend to be our constant companion. So the question is…which ego trap is yours? Do you lean on your technical skills when you should be focusing more on your leadership skills? Do you tend to surround yourself with people just like you? Or perhaps you underestimate how much you're being watched?

I recommend a two-part approach to diagnosing your personal ego traps.

- First, use your self-awareness to check in and identify the areas where your ego tends to flare up.
- Second, gather feedback from multiple sources.

Start by tuning into your own understanding of yourself. What are the high-ego behaviors that seem to come naturally or instinctively to you? Where do you tend to slip up when you are on autopilot? Maybe there is something you do that you know you shouldn't, like cut people off during conversations or avoid mingling with your frontline workers. It might even be something you rationalize, such as "We don't have time for the team to come up with their own answers—I have to jump in with ideas when I have them" or "The ground level folks don't want to spend time with the stuffed shirts." For an informal way to begin recognizing which ego trap or traps are most relevant for you, see the *Identifying Your Ego Traps* exercise in the appendix.

Once you have done your ego trap self-assessment, it's time to validate it with the help of a qualified coach who can gather feedback from others. At this point, your coach will ask a variety of people who work around you for feedback—formally, informally, or both—on your leadership performance.

It may feel a little uncomfortable at first. Who likes to put themselves at risk for criticism? Yet it's the most effective leaders who put a priority on gathering performance feedback. So as any discomfort or worries arise, try to remind yourself that it is far better to know than not to know. There is a peace of mind that comes with knowledge and understanding, especially when that knowledge and understanding allow you to proactively address feedback rather than guess how to improve your leadership effectiveness without any real data.

This is where the 360-degree feedback assessment comes in. As discussed in Ego Trap 1, the 360-degree assessment is a survey taken by multiple people who work with you, creating a full circle of feedback for you to consider. This tool may have a formal, written component for people to complete, as well as an informal, verbal piece in which the person conducting the assessment interviews these same people.

The cost is affordable and the time commitment is reasonable. The result is a baseline of information that you can use to gauge your current leadership performance and to identify areas for growth and improvement. After that, you can choose whether to continue working with an executive coach on an ongoing basis to address areas highlighted in the feedback and sharpen your EQ. Because we all have our personal biases, a qualified coach can help you cut through all the noise and zero in on areas for development that deliver the best results in the shortest time and offer tools for planning and measurement.

When you receive the results of the 360-degree feedback, plan to listen for common themes among responses. You may not have to respond to each and every comment, but if a pattern emerges among the answers, that's an area to explore more deeply. For example, the feedback from multiple sources might go something like this:

- "Sometimes it seems like Margot drifts in meetings."
- "Margot has a tendency to interrupt a lot."
- "Margot very quickly jumps to a conclusion before someone has a chance to give her all the information."
- "I don't think Margot always understands what I'm saying."

Although each statement is different, there is a common theme of poor listening skills. So it's a high-value area for Margot to key into. If she had only received one communication-related comment on her 360-degree assessment, it might not be something worth addressing immediately. Instead, we could take a wait-and-see approach before reacting to it. A coach can help the leader identify patterns that are worth addressing, as well as decide which pieces of feedback to set aside, at least for the moment. The 360-degree assessment is an invaluable tool that can help you discover those ego-based behaviors you didn't even know you were engaging in and bring to the surface behaviors you have rationalized, until now.

Just as you need to be patient with yourself, you may also need to be patient with your people. It may take time for them to notice that you've changed or to start to trust that the new you is going to stick around. Another variation you should be prepared for, others may sense the change in you and resist. That actually happened to Marty, whose team was so used to him rescuing them and jumping in to take over operational tasks that they got cranky when he started holding them accountable for doing their own work. They were used to the old Marty and were thrown off balance when the new Marty held them to a higher set of expectations and stepped back to give them more autonomy and responsibility. Marty held strong, though, and gave his team time to adjust—and they did. Once they got comfortable with their new roles, they found their jobs more rewarding and learned to enjoy the respect that Marty now gave them.

The ongoing effort of applying EQ is like anything you do as a leader. If earnings are good in quarter 1, you know you don't go on a three-month vacation in quarter 2, but instead see how you can continue or expand these earnings into Q2, Q3, and Q4. When you start to see the marketing campaign moving market share, you don't abandon your investment and let it ride on momentum. Instead, you maintain your course of action and see what the maximum return on your investment could be. Similarly, your efforts to avoid the ego traps and to exercise high EQ need to be consistent and long term to be effective. Fortunately, the benefits will be felt throughout multiple areas of the business and your organization, so the time and focus you put toward sharpening and maintaining your EQ will be well worth it. Here are just some of the benefits:

- When you listen to feedback from others, you gain high-quality information and make better decisions.
- When you start valuing your leadership skills as much as your technical skills, you open the space for others to add value and mine opportunities that were previously stifled.
- If you surround yourself with different viewpoints, you design better competitive responses and build stronger strategies.
- When you start letting go of control and letting people do what they need to do, you will gain time and energy to focus on company strategy, industry landscape, and your competition.
- When you tune in to your downstream impact, you are better able to identify which ideas to have your team implement right away and which initiatives to table or rank lower on the priority chain.
- If you realize that you are being watched, you can model the culture you want to see throughout your organization.

- When you are humbled by spending time with your frontline employees and consider the impact of what you are asking them to do every day, it gives you a sense of purpose as you reconnect with your organization's mission from the ground up.
- When you learn to exercise your EQ over the long term and avoid sliding back into the ego traps, you become a magnet for talent.

The unknown is always scarier than the known. By raising your self-awareness and discovering what is over your shoulder, you can ultimately find more peace of mind.

EQ Antidote: Recognizing, Reading, and Responding

As suggested throughout the book, every change initiative must start with a look within. Dust off your self-awareness and *recognize* what's going on inside you in response to your environment and interactions. To ensure high-EQ performance, take regular self-check-in breaks throughout the day—even for sixty seconds—to identify your own mood, emotions, and motivations. Consider how these moods, etc., might impact those around you.

Next, turn on your empathy monitor and take some time to *read* others. Again, this might involve only a minute or two of reflection—the important thing is to pause and ask, "How might the people I'm leading feel in this particular situation?" When you read others, it helps to consider what their emotional state might be in a given moment based on what you know about them and their background. A person's facial expressions, body language, and commentary can all help you piece together their emotional state. It's okay, too, to ask, "How are you feeling right now, having heard that news?" or "Now that you know about this policy change, what's going through your mind?" Having EQ involves tuning in as best as you can, and then having the humility and interest to ask for additional information about the other person or people when you need it.

Lastly, *respond* with self-control. Those in positions of great authority must have the greatest self-control. The stakes are the highest and the rewards the richest.

Your people expect disciplined leadership and they need you to provide a model for them. They need a leader who has the self-possession to edit the random statements and hurtful comments that can disrupt or upset others. They need the space that only you can create for them by being open-minded and tempered in your responses.

The three Rs are meant to provide you with a relatively simple way to remember how to keep your EQ strong throughout the day—prompting you to *recognize* your own emotional state, *read* others, and *respond* appropriately and with presence of mind. And yet the truth is that it is not always easy to exercise high EQ in the moment or to keep it as a priority in your thinking. Working with an executive coach, having honest conversations with a group of your peers, and cherry-picking the most relevant concepts in this book to review from time to time are just some of the ways that you can keep your commitment to maintaining high emotional intelligence strong. Remember, too, that the process of sharpening and reengaging your EQ skills may take some time, but your increased effectiveness is well worth the effort.

In a Nutshell

As a leader, you are always subject to factors that you can't control, whether it's the supply of your raw materials, competitive moves, regulatory requirements, or any number of other unwelcome surprises. What you *can* control is how you interact with your team—whether you lead from an unconscious place driven by ego or instead lead with EQ at the fore, consciously exercising your self-awareness, empathy, and self-control. It takes some effort to be an emotionally intelligent leader, but it doesn't have to be all-consuming. What's more, you don't have to change who you are.

The goal is not to become someone you are not. In fact, people can usually tell if you are being insincere; on the flip side, they respond best to you when you bring your strengths to the table. So the goal really is to retain your strengths while being aware of the few areas where ego may tend to trip you up. Once you have heightened this awareness, you can shift your sail ever so slightly when needed—doing the small things when they matter—and then watch as the individuals around you begin to respond more positively and the organization shifts into a powerful new direction.

I often tell my clients that it's the little things that really matter. Consider any of the following simple ideas to lessen ego and maximize EQ, with a surprisingly big payoff.

- An executive goes to someone else's office for a meeting instead of having the person come to hers. *Payoff: Employees see that the executive is willing to put forth effort and get out of her comfort zone.*
- A leader sits at the lunchroom table with assembly-line workers instead of eating in the corporate dining room. *Payoff: The leader sends the message that he is genuinely interested in getting to know people in the company.*
- The president stands at the grill during the company picnic and makes the hotdogs instead of waiting to be served. *Payoff: Demonstrating servant leadership increases the leader's approachability and improves communication.*
- The CEO takes time to visit with frontline workers after an awards ceremony rather than dashing off to his next appointment. *Payoff: Spending time with staff reinforces the executive's appreciation of extraordinary individual and team effort and her commitment to organizational values.*

What simple adjustments are you ready and willing to make? Remember, it's not about changing who you are, but instead opening your eyes to some of your blind spots and being courageous enough to make a few small—but incredibly powerful—changes. It's those simple course corrections that can put you and your organization on even stronger footing. And who knows what good things can happen from there?

Appendix
Identifying Your Ego Blind Spots

Check the box next to each of the following scenarios that describes you at work. Then consider how you could gather more data and address your potential ego-related blind spots.

Ego Trap 1—Ignoring Feedback You Don't Like

☐ You take the fact that you don't receive much negative or constructive feedback as a sign that you are doing your job as a leader really well and don't need to focus on your own leadership development.

☐ You assume, without testing, that if your team is honest with you about operational issues that they can also be relied upon to give you candid feedback about how you are doing as a leader.

☐ You do not regularly ask your team for feedback, and when people attempt to give you some form of feedback, you rebuff or ignore them rather than inviting them to share more.

☐ You think secretly to yourself: "If they don't like what I'm doing, they can go get a job somewhere else!"

Ego Trap 2—Believing Your Technical Skills Trump Your Leadership Skills

☐ You consider being a subject-matter expert enough to make you a great leader and feel this excuses you from wasting your time accommodating people.

☐ You listen in meetings for chances to jump in and share your expertise or catch others in a mistake rather than letting them work through the issue at their own pace and honoring their process, knowledge, and creativity.

☐ You take great pride in having been told by others that you are a "genius" at what you do while ignoring or minimizing feedback that you could improve at some of the "softer" leadership skills like listening, empowerment, or communication skills.

☐ You think being a leader means being the "fixer."

Ego Trap 3—Surrounding Yourself with More of You

☐ You don't have anyone in your inner circle who has a work or communication style opposite your own.

☐ Decisions among the executive team are made quickly and easily with minimal challenging viewpoints. (Although, you gotta love those short meetings!)

☐ Your executive leadership team lacks diversity (e.g., all are white males in their 50's).

☐ Challengers in the company are often ostracized, labeled as naysayers, or seen as "just not team players."

☐ Your company lacks a formal, structured interviewing and selection process, and managers, including you, have the latitude to hire on "gut feel" with little or no evidence of competency or indication that the person's skills match the job's requirements.

Ego Trap 4—Not Letting Go of Control

☐ You have more than ten direct reports.[1]

☐ You cannot help but get involved in seemingly minor details "just for peace of mind."

- ☐ You spend much of your time focused inward, on company operations, and very little looking outward at the industry or business landscape.
- ☐ When you are away from the office, decisions grind to a halt or it seems nothing gets done until you return, validating, of course, that you are indeed indispensable and your senior team is helpless without you.
- ☐ You see yourself as the ultimate quality-control inspector.
- ☐ You feel people need very detailed instructions in order to perform at their best.

Ego Trap 5—Being Blind to Your Downstream Impact

- ☐ You routinely ask people to help you with a task, though it isn't their job, because you know they will get it done.
- ☐ You never hear "No" in answer to a request and are rarely asked to negotiate a deadline.
- ☐ You call last minute-meetings, assuming that everyone will clear their calendar for you, and they all show up.
- ☐ Before making a requested change, you don't consider how easy or difficult it will be to accomplish at *someone else's* level.
- ☐ You allow things to fall completely off the grid, then suddenly request an update.

Ego Trap 6 —Underestimating How Much You're Being Watched

- ☐ You think that there are different rules for executives than for everyone else.
- ☐ At a company function you sit with your small circle of peers or direct reports instead of using it as an opportunity to meet employees you don't know.
- ☐ You believe it's okay to behave like everyone else at company meetings because it makes you "one of the guys."

☐ You chronically put scheduling priorities over opportunities to spend time with employees.

Ego Trap 7—Losing Touch with the Front Line Experience
☐ You have employees come to your office for a meeting instead of going to theirs.
☐ You don't periodically spend time working alongside employees for a "day in the life" experience.
☐ You have employees working in locations you have never visited. (Anywhere in the *world* you ask? Yes, anywhere in the *world*.)
☐ You always fly first class or on the company jet, while your travel policy requires that all employees fly coach.

Ego Trap 8—Relapsing Back to Your Old Ways
☐ You find yourself operating on autopilot, not making mindful choices in interactions with others.
☐ You think you have "fixed things" and don't need to worry about having EQ goals anymore. You see these changes as tasks to be checked off your list rather than as an attitude to be exercised over the long term.
☐ You see certain audiences as worthy of your best efforts while others, in your view, are not.
☐ On good days you demonstrate high EQ but feel justified in letting it slide on bad days. Having high EQ doesn't mean I have to be perfect, right?

Endnotes

Introduction

1. *New York Times*, "Times Topics: Oil Spills," last modified August 17, 2011, http://topics.nytimes.com/top/reference/timestopics/subjects/o/oil_spills/index.html.
2. Maev Kennedy, "BP Chief's Weekend Sailing Trip Stokes Anger at Oil Company: Pictures of Tony Hayward Yachting at the Isle of Wight Billed as a PR Nightmare and Insulting to Those Affected by the Oil Slick," *The Guardian*, June 20, 2010, accessed March 4, 2013, http://www.guardian.co.uk/business/2010/jun/20/tony-hayward-bp.
3. *New York Times*, "Times Topics: Rupert Murdoch," last modified December 3, 2012, http://topics.nytimes.com/top/reference/timestopics/people/m/rupert_murdoch/index.html.
4. Nick Davies and Amelia Hill, "Missing Milly Dowler's Voicemail was Hacked by *News of the World*," *The Guardian*, July 4, 2011, accessed March 4, 2013, http://www.guardian.co.uk/uk/2011/jul/04/milly-dowler-voicemail-hacked-news-of-world.
5. William D Cohan and Bethany McLean, "Jamie Dimon on the Line," *Vanity Fair*, November 2012, 174–179, 199–203.
6. Susan Adams, "The Worst CEO Screw-Ups of 2012," *Forbes,* December 19, 2012, accessed March 4, 2013, http://www.forbes.com/sites/susanadams/2012/12/19/the-worst-ceo-screw-ups-of-2012/.
7. Daniel Goleman, "What Makes a Leader?" *Harvard Business Review,* 2004, accessed March 4, 2013, http://hbr.org/2004/01/what-makes-a-leader/ar/1.
8. Daniel Goleman, *Working with Emotional Intelligence* (New York: Bantam Books, 1998). 317.
9 Nikki Blacksmith and Jim Harter, "Majority of American Workers Not Engaged in Their Jobs: Highly Educated and Middle-Aged Employees among

the Least Likely to Be Engaged," *Gallup Well-Being,* October 28, 2011, accessed March 4, 2013, http://www.gallup.com/poll/150383/Majority-American -Workers-Not-Engaged-Jobs.aspx?utm_source=email-a-friend&utm_ medium=email&utm_campaign=sharing&utm_content=morelink.

10. Reuven Bar-On, "A Broad Definition of Emotional-Social Intelligence According to the Bar-On Model," Reuven Bar-On.org, last modified April 18, 2007, http://www.reuvenbaron.org/bar-on-model/essay.php?i=2.

11. In this book, I opt to use the terms *emotional intelligence (EI)* and *emotional intelligence quotient (EQ)* synonymously, leaning toward the more frequent use of *EQ* because it is a term readily recognized and understood by mainstream audiences and thus meets the practical needs of our intended audience.

12. Mark Slaski and Susan Cartwright, "Health, Performance, and Emotional Intelligence: An Exploratory Study of Retail Managers," *Stress and Health* 18 (2002): 63–38.

13. Multi-Health Systems (MHI), "Emotional Intelligence and Return on Investment: Return on Your EQ-i Investment," accessed from http:// downloads.mhs.com/ei/MHS_Brief_ROI.pdf.

14. Geetu Bharwaney, Reuven Bar-On, and Adèle MacKinlay, *EQ and the Bottom Line: Emotional Intelligence Increases Individual Occupational Performance, Leadership and Organisational Productivity* (Bedfordshire MK: Ei World Limited, 2011). 7.

15. *Merriam–Webster Dictionary,* accessed March 4, 2013, http://www.merriam -webster.com/dictionary/egotism.

16. Travis Bradberry, Jean Greaves, and Patrick Lencioni, *Emotional Intelligence 2.0. (*San Diego: TalentSmart, 2009). 235.

17. Ram Charan, "Ending the CEO Succession Crisis," *Harvard Business Review,* February 2005, http://hbr.org/2005/02/ending-the-ceo-succession-crisis/ ar/1.

18. Ray B. Williams, "Wired for Success: How to Fulfill Your Potential—Why CEOs Fail—Execution?" *Psychology Today,* May 2, 2009, accessed March 4, 2013, http://www.psychologytoday.com/blog/wired-success/200905/why -ceos-fail-execution.

19. "Frequently Asked Questions," Small Business Administration, last updated September 2012, http://www.sba.gov/sites/default/files/FINAL%20FAQ% 202012%20Sept%202012%20web.pdf.

20. Erik Schatzker, Dawn Kopecki, Bradley Keoun, and Christine Harper, "Jamie Dimon's Risky Business," *Bloomberg Businessweek,* June 14, 2012, accessed March 4, 2013, http://www.businessweek.com/articles/2012-06-14/jamie -dimons-risky-business#p1.

21. Antoine Gara, "JPMorgan's Dimon Says He Couldn't Spot 'London Whale,'" June 12, 2012, accessed March 4, 2013, http://www.thestreet

.com/story/11578667/1/jpmorgans-dimon-says-he-couldnt-spot-london-whale.html.

22. As cited earlier, William D. Cohan and Bethany McLean, "Jamie Dimon on the Line," *Vanity Fair*, November 2012, 174–179, 199–203.

23. Gillian Tett, *Fool's Gold: The Inside Story of J.P. Morgan and How Wall St. Greed Corrupted Its Bold Dream and Created a Financial Catastrophe*, (New York: Free Press, 2010). 107.

24. Erik Schatzker, Dawn Kopecki, Bradley Keoun, and Christine Harper, "Jamie Dimon's Risky Business," *Bloomberg Businessweek*, June 14, 2012, accessed March 4, 2013, http://www.businessweek.com/articles/2012-06-14/jamie-dimons-risky-business#p1.

25. We now know, thanks to Daniel Goleman and colleagues, that a strong EQ is made up of self-regulation, flexibility, stress tolerance, and influence. I have found in my work with busy executives that it is most efficient to focus on just three of these EQ traits: self-awareness, empathy, and self-control. With these three EQ tools under your belt, you will have the essentials needed to build a happy productive team and develop an organizational culture that thrives under your leadership.

Ego Trap 1

1. Louis N. Quast, "Prevent Top Leader Derailment," *Talent Management Magazine* (October 2012): 42.

2. Allan H. Church, "Managerial Self-Awareness in High-Performing Individuals in Organizations," *Journal of Applied Psychology* 82, no. 2 (1997): 281–292.

3. L. E. Atwater and F. J. Yammarino, "Does Self-Other Agreement on Leadership Perceptions Moderate the Validity of Leadership and Performance Predictions?" *Personnel Psychology* 45 (1992): 141–164.

4. Daniel Goleman, "What Makes a Leader?" *Harvard Business Review,* January 2004, accessed March 4, 2013, http://hbr.org/2004/01/what-makes-a-leader/ar/1.

5. "What Predicts Executive Success," *Talent Management,* (September 9, 2010): 2, accessed March 4, 2013, http://talentmgt.com/articles/view/what_predicts_executive_success/1.

6. Self-awareness was measured based on the executives' answers to in-depth interviews and interviews of the executives' bosses.

7. Daniel Goleman, Richard Boyatzis, and Annie McKee, *Primal Leadership: Learning to Lead with Emotional Intelligence* (Boston: Harvard Business Review Press, 2004), 92.

8. Fabio Sala, "It's Lonely at the Top: Executives' Emotional Intelligence Self (Mis) Perceptions," Consortium for Research on Emotional Intelligence

in Organizations, Hay/McBer, 2001, accessed March 4, 2013, www.eicon sortium.org.

9. Names and some details have been changed throughout the book to maintain clients' anonymity.

10. Netscape Editors, "No. 1 Reason People Quit Their Jobs," *AOL News,* accessed March 4, 2013, http://webcenters.netscape.compuserve.com/whatsnew/package.jsp?name=fte/quitjobs/quitjobs&floc=wn-dx.

11. James Conway and Allen Huffcutt, "Psychometric Properties of Multi-Source Performance Ratings: A Meta-Analysis of Subordinate, Supervisor, Peer and Self-Ratings," *Human Performance* 10, no. 4 (1977): 331–360, as cited in Daniel Goleman, Richard Boyatzis, and Annie McKee, *Primal Leadership: Learning to Lead with Emotional Intelligence* (*Harvard Business Review Press*, 2004): 92.

Ego Trap 2

1. Boris Groysberg, L. Kevin Kelly, and Bryan MacDonald, "The New Path to the C-Suite," *Harvard Business Review*, March 2011, accessed March 4, 2013, http://hbr.org/2005/02/ending-the-ceo-succession-crisis/ar/1.

2. Leadership IQ, "Why New Hires Fail," Leadership IQ Study, September 20, 2005, accessed March 4, 2013, http://www.leadershipiq.com/materials/Hiring_For_Attitude_1.pdf.

3. Interestingly, research by Martin Seligman shows that optimism (one of the key EQ skills) is considered to be a liability for attorneys like Gary. As a result, this group is trained to think in terms of win–lose, rather than win–win, which is fine for legal matters but not for excelling as a leader at the executive level. See Martin Seligman, *Authentic Happiness: Using the New Positive Psychology to Realize Your Potential for Lasting Fulfillment* (Atria Books, 2003).

Ego Trap 3

1. Peter Drucker, "Drucker on Management: There's More Than One Kind of Team," *Wall Street Journal* (November 18, 2009), accessed March 4, 2013, http://online.wsj.com/article/SB10001424052748704204304574544312916277426.html.

2. Jon R. Katzenbach and Douglas K. Smith, *The Wisdom of Teams: Creating the High-Performance Organization* (HarperBusiness: 2003).

3. Vicky Elmer, "Now Hiring. Wanted? Someone Just Like Me," *CNN Money,* November 29, 2012, accessed March 4, 2013, http://management.fortune.cnn.com/2012/11/29/now-hiring-wanted-someone-just-like-me/.

4. Audrey J. Lee, "Unconscious Bias Theory in Employment Discrimination Litigation," accessed March 4, 2013, http://www.law.harvard.edu/stu dents/orgs/crcl/vol40_2/lee.pdf.
5. Claudio Fernández-Aráoz, "Hiring Without Firing," *Harvard Business Review,* July 1999, accessed March 4, 2013, http://hbr.org/1999/07/hiring-without-firing/ar/1.
6. Audrey J. Lee, "Unconscious Bias Theory in Employment Discrimination Litigation," accessed March 4, 2013, http://www.law.harvard.edu/students /orgs/crcl/vol40_2/lee.pdf.
7. "Where's the Diversity in Fortune 500 CEOs?" *Diversity Inc.* magazine, accessed March 5, 2013, http://www.diversityinc.com/facts/wheres-the -diversity-in-fortune-500-ceos/.
8. Karen Boman, "Lack of Diversity Prevents O&G Companies from Seeing All Risks," *Rigzone*, August 7, 2012, accessed March 5, 2013, http://www. rigzone.com/news/oil_gas/a/119849/Lack_of_Diversity_Prevents_OG_ Companies_from_Seeing_All_Risks.
9. Ibid.
10. Companies on the All Country World Index (MSCI ACWI) experienced a rise in the proportion of women on the board from 41 percent at the end of 2005 to 59 percent at the end of 2011, according to the previous article by Karen Boman.
11. "Results of Menendez's Major Fortune 500 Diversity Survey: Representation of Women and Minorities on Corporate Boards Still Lags Far Behind National Population," August 4, 2010, accessed March 5, http:// www.menendez.senate.gov/newsroom/press/results-of-menendezs -major-fortune-500-diversity survey-representation-of-women-and -minorities-on-corporate-boards-still-lags-far-behind-national-population.
12. William D. Cohan and Bethany McLean, "Jamie Dimon on the Line," *Vanity Fair*, November 2012, 174–179, 199–203.
13. Ibid.
14. Ibid.
15. Ibid.

Ego Trap 4

1. Ron Ashkenas, "Why People Micromanage," *HBR Blog Network*, November 15, 2011, accessed March 5, 2013, http://blogs.hbr.org/ashkenas/2011/11/ why-people-micromanage.html.
2. Alison Stein Wellner, "Who Can You Trust? Why So Many Entrepreneurs Have Trouble Delegating," *Inc.* magazine, October 1, 2004, accessed March 5, 2013, http://www.inc.com/magazine/20041001/managing.html.

3. Gary L. Neilson and Julie Wulf, "How Many Direct Reports?" *Harvard Business Review*, April 2012, accessed March 5, 2013, http://hbr.org/2012/04/how-many-direct-reports/ar/1.

4. Robert Greenleaf, *The Servant as Leader*, (Westfield: Robert K. Greenleaf Center, 1982). 9.

5. Ron Roberts, "How To Gain Control By Letting Go," *Fast Company*, July 8, 2012, accessed March 5, 2013, http://www.fastcompany.com/1841995/how-gain-control-letting-go.

6. Jillian Berman, "Jamie Dimon's Bonus Could Be Hurt By London Whale Loss," *The Huffington Post*, January 13, 2012, accessed March 5, 2013, http://www.huffingtonpost.com/2013/01/13/jamie-dimon-bonus_n_2468004.html.

7. Associated Press, "BP Feared Spill of 3.4 Million Gallons a Day," January 28, 2012, accessed March 5, 2013, http://www.nytimes.com/2012/01/29/us/bp-feared-gulf-oil-spill-rate-of-3-4-million-gallons-a-day.html?_r=0.

Ego Trap 5

1. Shane Perrault, "Entrepreneurs with ADHD: How Leaders (and Aspiring Leaders) with ADHD Can Harness Their Creativity and Increase Their Productivity," *Psychology Today,* September 16, 2009, accessed March 6, 2013, http://www.psychologytoday.com/blog/entrepreneurs-adhd/200909/7-habits-highly-successful-entrepreneurs-adhd.

Ego Trap 6

1. Michael E. Porter and Nitin Nohria, "What Is Leadership? The CEO's Role in Large, Complex Organizations," in *Handbook of Leadership Theory and Practice: A Harvard Business School Centennial Colloquium,* edited by Nitin Nohria and Rakesh Khurana (Boston: Harvard Business Press: 2010). 27.

2. Jim Kouzes and Barry Pozner, "The Five Practices of Exemplary Leadership Model," The Leadership Challenge, accessed March 6, 2013, http://www.leadershipchallenge.com/about-section-our-approach.aspx.

3. Michael E. Porter and Nitin Nohria, "What Is Leadership? The CEO's Role in Large, Complex Organizations," in *Handbook of Leadership Theory and Practice: A Harvard Business School Centennial Colloquium,* edited by Nitin Nohria and Rakesh Khurana (Boston: Harvard Business Press: 2010). 27.

4. Daniel Goleman, "What Makes a Leader?," *Harvard Business Review*, January 2004, accessed March 4, 2013, http://hbr.org/2004/01/what -makes-a-leader/ar/1.

5. Jim Kouzes and Barry Pozner, "The Five Practices of Exemplary Leadership Model," The Leadership Challenge, accessed March 6, 2013, http://www.leadershipchallenge.com/about-section-our-approach.aspx.

6. Daniel Goleman, "What Makes a Leader?" *Harvard Business Review*, January 2004, accessed March 4, 2013, http://hbr.org/2004/01/what -makes-a-leader/ar/1.

Ego Trap 7

1. Alan Snel, "Subway: Lessons Learned While Undercover," *Restaurant News*, November 20, 2010, accessed March 6, 2013, http://nrn.com/archive/ subway-lessons-learned-while-undercover.

2. Jonathan Berr, "Choice Hotels CEO Cleans up His Act on 'Undercover Boss,'" *Daily Finance*, September 27, 2010, accessed March 6, 2013, http://www.dailyfinance.com/2010/09/27/choice-hotels-ceo-stephen-joyce -undercover-boss/.

3. "About Undercover Boss," CBS, accessed March 6, 2013,http://www.cbs .com/shows/undercover_boss/about/.

4. Quoted from "'Undercover Boss': American Seafoods CEO Struggles as a Deckhand" video. *Huff Post TV*, accessed March 6, 2013, http://www .huffingtonpost.com/2012/02/27/undercover-boss-american-seafoods -ceo-video n 1303268.html).

5. Rodney Ho, "Recap of 'Undercover Boss' featuring Atlanta-based Hooters," *Access Atlanta*, February 14, 2010, accessed March 6, 2013, http://blogs.ajc .com/radio-tv-talk/2010/02/14/recap-of-undercover-boss-featuring-atlanta -based-hooters/.

6. "'Undercover Boss': American Seafoods CEO Struggles as a Deckhand" video. *Huff Post TV*, accessed March 6, 2013, http://www.huffingtonpost .com/2012/02/27/undercover-boss-american-seafoods-ceo-video_ n 1303268.html.

7. Joanne Ostrow, "Sara Bittorf, Boston Market Executive from Golden, Is 'Undercover Boss,'" *Denver Post,* January 29, 2013, accessed March 6, 2013, http://blogs.denverpost.com/ostrow/2013/01/29/sara-bittorf-boston -market-undercover-boss-show/12604/.

8. Alan Snel, "Subway: Lessons Learned While Undercover," *Restaurant News*, November 20, 2010, accessed March 6, 2013, http://nrn.com/archive/ subway-lessons-learned-while-undercover.

9. Trip Mickel, "NASCAR Executive on "Undercover Boss," *Sporting News Nascar*, October 20, 2010, accessed March 6, 2013, http://aol.sportingnews.com/nascar/story/2010-10-20/nascar-executive-on-undercover-boss.

10. CNBC, "Tony Hsieh. I am American Business" [Producer notes for video], accessed March 6, 2013, http://www.cnbc.com/id/100000559/Tony_Hsieh.

11. Steven Rosenbaum, "The Happiness Culture: Zappos Isn't a Company—It's a Mission," *Fast Company*, June 4, 2010, accessed March 10, 2013, http://www.fastcompany.com/1657030/happiness-culture-zappos-isnt-company-its-mission.

12. Scott Powers, "Walt Disney Co. Ends Fiscal 2012 with Record Revenue, Profit, Earnings per Share," *Orlando Sentinel,* November 2012, accessed March 6, 2013, http://articles.orlandosentinel.com/2012-11-08/news/os-disney-earnings-4th-quarter-20121108_1_iger-record-revenue-theme-parks.

13. J.S., "The Ratio of CEO to Worker Compensation: Are They Worth It?" *The Economist*, May 8, 2012, accessed March 6, 2013, http://www.economist.com/blogs/graphicdetail/2012/05/ratio-ceo-worker-compensation.

14. Kevin Kruse, "Employee Engagement Research: Master List of 29 Studies," September 18, 2012, accessed March 6, 2013, http://kevinkruse.com/employee-engagement-research-master-list-of-29-studies.

15. Stanley Reed, "Tony Hayward Gets His Life Back," *New York Times*, September 1, 2012, accessed March 6, 2013, http://www.nytimes.com/2012/09/02/business/tony-hayward-former-bp-chief-returns-to-oil.html?pagewanted=all&_r=0.

Ego Trap 8

1. *Merriam-Webster Dictionary*, accessed March 6, 2013, http://www.merriam-webster.com/dictionary/credibility.

2. *Wikipedia,* accessed March 6, 2013 http://en.wikipedia.org/wiki/Credibility.

3. Stephen M. R. Covey, *The Speed of Trust: The One Thing that Changes Everything* (New York: Free Press, 2008), 45.

Conclusion

1. David Rock and Jeffrey Schwartz, "The Neuroscience of Leadership," *Strategy + Business*, May 30, 2006, 5, accessed March 6, 2013, http://www.strategy-business.com/article/06207?pg=4.

2. David Rock, "*Your Brain at Work: Strategies for Overcoming Distraction, Regaining Focus, and Working Smarter All Day Long (*New York: HarperBusiness, 2009). 225.

Appendix

1. Gary L. Neilson and Julie Wulf, "How Many Direct Reports?" *Harvard Business Review*, April 2012, accessed March 6, 2013, http://hbr.org/2012/04/how-many-direct-reports/ar/1.

References

Susan Adams, "The Worst CEO Screw-Ups of 2012." *Forbes,* December 19, 2012, http://www.forbes.com/sites/susanadams/2012/12/19/the-worst-ceo-screw-ups-of-2012/

Ron Ashkenas, "Why People Micromanage." *HBR Blog,* November 15, 2011, http://blogs.hbr.org/ashkenas/2011/11/why-people-micromanage.html.

L. E. Atwater and F. J. Yammarino, "Does Self-Other Agreement on Leadership Perceptions Moderate the Validity of Leadership and Performance Predictions?." *Personnel Psychology* 45 (1992): 141-164.

Claudio Fernández-Aráoz, "Hiring Without Firing." *Harvard Business Review,* July 1999.

Jillian Berman, "Jamie Dimon's Bonus Could Be Hurt By London Whale Loss." *The Huffington Post,* January 13, 2012, http://www.huffingtonpost.com/2013/01/13/jamie-dimon-bonus_n_2468004.html

Jonathan Berr, "Choice Hotels CEO Cleans up His Act on 'Undercover Boss.'" *Daily Finance,* September 27, 2010.

Geetu Bharwaney, Reuven Bar-On, and Adèle MacKinlay, *EQ and the Bottom Line: Emotional Intelligence Increases Individual Occupational Performance, Leadership and Organisational Productivity* (Bedfordshire: Ei World Limited, 2011).

Nikki Blacksmith and Jim Harter, "Majority of American Workers Not Engaged in Their Jobs: Highly Educated and Middle-Aged Employees among the Least Likely to Be Engaged." *Gallup,* October 28, 2011, http://www.gallup.com/poll/150383/majority-american-workers-not-engaged-jobs.aspx

Karen Boman, "Lack of Diversity Prevents O&G Companies from Seeing All Risks." *Rigzone,* August 7, 2012, http://www.rigzone.com/news/oil_gas/a/119849/Lack_of_Diversity_Prevents_OG_Companies_from_Seeing_All_Risks.

Travis Bradberry, Jean Greaves, and Patrick Lencioni, *Emotional Intelligence 2.0.* (San Diego: TalentSmart, 2009).

Susan Cartwright and Mark Slaski, "Health, Performance, and Emotional Intelligence: An Exploratory Study of Retail Managers." *Stress and Health* 18 (2002): 63-68.

Ram Charan, "Ending the CEO Succession Crisis." *Harvard Business Review,* February 2005.

Allan H. Church, "Managerial Self-Awareness in High-Performing Individuals in Organizations." *Journal of Applied Psychology* 82 (1997): 281-292.

William D. Cohan and Bethany McLean, "Jamie Dimon on the Line." *Vanity Fair* November 2012, http://www.vanityfair.com/business/2012/11/jamie-dimon-tom-brady-hang-in-there

Nick Davies and Amelia Hill, "Missing Milly Dowler's Voicemail was Hacked by *News of the World.*" *The Guardian,* July 4, 2011.

Peter Drucker, "Drucker on Management: There's More Than One Kind of Team." *Wall Street Journal,* November 18, 2009.

Vicky Elmer, "Now Hiring. Wanted? Someone Just Like Me." *CNN Money,* November 29, 2012.

Antoine Gara, "JPMorgan's Dimon Says He Couldn't Spot 'London Whale,'." *The Street,* June, 12, 2012, http://www.thestreet.com/story/11578667/1/jpmorgans-dimon-says-he-couldnt-spot-london-whale.html

Ketaki Gokhale, "Gartner Raises IT Spending Growth Projection on Cloud Services," *Bloomberg,* July 9, 2012.

Robert Greenleaf, *The Servant as Leader.* (Westfield, IN: Robert K. Greenleaf Center, 1982).

Boris Grovsberg, Kevin Kelly, and Bryan MacDonald, "The New Path to the C Suite." *Harvard Business Review,* March 2011.

Daniel Goleman, "What Makes a Leader?." *Harvard Business Review,* January 2004.

Daniel Goleman, *Emotional Intelligence: Why It Can Matter More Than IQ?.* (New York: Bantam Books, 1995).

Daniel Goleman, Richard Boyatzis, and Annie McKee, *Primal Leadership: Learning to Lead with Emotional Intelligence.* (Boston: Harvard Business Review Press, 2004).

Harold S. Kushner, *When Bad Things Happen to Good People,* (New York: Anchor, 2004).

Rodney Ho, "Recap of 'Undercover Boss' featuring Atlanta-based Hooters." *Access Atlanta,* February 14, 2010, http://blogs.ajc.com/radio-tv-talk/2010/02/14/recap-of-undercover-boss-featuring-atlanta-based-hooters/.

Maev Kennedy, "BP chief's weekend sailing trip stokes anger at oil company." *The Guardian,* June 20, 2010, http://www.theguardian.com/business/2010/jun/20/tony-hayward-bp.

Jon R. Katzenbach and Douglas K. Smith, *The Wisdom of Teams: Creating the High Performance Organization,* HarperBusiness: 2003.

The Leadership Challenge. "The Five Practices of Exemplary Leadership Model." Acessed August 2, 2013, http://www.leadershipchallenge.com/About-section-Our-Approach.aspx

Kevin Kruse, "Employee Engagement Research: Master List of 29 Studies" Last modified September 18, 2012, http://kevinkruse.com/employee-engagement-research-master-list-of-29-studies/.

Audrey J. Lee, "Unconscious Bias Theory in Employment Discrimination Litigation," *Harvard Civil Rights – Civil Liberties Review* 40 (2005): 481-488.

Trip Mickel, "NASCAR Executive on "Undercover Boss," *Sporting News Nascar,* October 20, 2010, http://www.sportingnews.com/nascar/story/2010-10-20/nascar-executive-on-undercover-boss

Gary L. Neilson and Julie Wulf, "How Many Direct Reports?" *Harvard Business Review,* April 2012.

Joanne Ostrow, "Sara Bittorf, Boston Market Executive from Golden, Is 'Undercover Boss,'" *Denver Post,* January 29, 2013, http://blogs.denverpost.com/ostrow/2013/01/29/sara-bittorf-boston-market-undercover-boss-show/12604/

Shane Perrault, "Entrepreneurs with ADHD: How Leaders (and Aspiring Leaders) with ADHD Can Harness Their Creativity and Increase Their Productivity." *Psychology Today,* September 16, 2009.

Michael E. Porter and Nitin Nohria, "What Is Leadership? The CEO's Role in Large, Complex Organizations." from *Handbook of Leadership Theory and Practice: A Harvard Business School Centennial Colloquium.* (Boston: Harvard Business Press, 2010) 433-473.

Scott Powers, "Walt Disney Co. Ends Fiscal 2012 with Record Revenue, Profit, Earnings per Share." *Orlando Sentinel,* November 2012.

Louis N. Quast, "Prevent Top Leader Derailment." *Talent Management Magazine,* October 2012.

Stanley Reed, "Tony Hayward Gets His Life Back." *New York Times,* September 1, 2012.

David Rock and Jeffrey Schwartz, "The Neuroscience of Leadership." *Strategy + Business,* May 30, 2006.

David Rock, *Your Brain at Work: Strategies for Overcoming Distraction, Regaining Focus, and Working Smarter All Day Long.* (New York: Harper Business, 2009).

Steven Rosenbaum, "The Happiness Culture: Zappos Isn't a Company—It's a Mission." *Fast Company,* June 4, 2010.

Ron Roberts, "How To Gain Control By Letting Go." *Fast Company* July 8, 2012.

Fabio Sala, "It's Lonely at the Top: Executives' Emotional Intelligence Self [Mis] Perceptions." (Consortium for Research on Emotional Intelligence in Organizations, 2001).

Gary Stern, "Company Training Programs: What Are They Really Worth?." *CNNMoney*, May 27, 20011.

Alan Snel, "Subway: Lessons Learned While Undercover." *Restaurant News*, November 20, 2010.

Erik Schatzker, Dawn Kopecki, Bradley Keoun, and Christine Harper, "Jamie Dimon's Risky Business," *Bloomberg Businessweek*, June 14, 2012.

J.S., "The Ratio of CEO to Worker Compensation: Are They Worth It?" *The Economist,* May 8, 2012, http://www.economist.com/blogs/graphicdetail/2012/05/ratio-ceo-worker-compensation.

Gillian Tett, *Fool's Gold: The Inside Story of J.P. Morgan and How Wall St. Greed Corrupted Its Bold Dream and Created a Financial Catastrophe.* (New York: Free Press, 2010.

Ray B. Williams, "Why CEOs Fail—Execution?." *Psychology Today,* May 2, 2009, http://www.psychologytoday.com/blog/wired-success/200905/why-ceos-fail-execution.

Alison Stein Wellner, "Who Can You Trust? Why So Many Entrepreneurs Have Trouble Delegating." *Inc.*, October 1, 2004, http://www.inc.com/magazine/20041001/managing.html.

Index

About the Author

Jen Shirkani wrote *Ego vs EQ* to help leaders help themselves. As an executive coach, she takes the science of EQ (emotional intelligence) and brings it to practical application for the senior executive or business owner who not only wants to survive, but thrive. She has over twenty years of experience working with Fortune 500 organizations and family-owned companies helping leaders leverage the power of EQ. She was born and raised in Southern California and holds a Master's Degree in Organizational Leadership. When not with her two daughters, she enjoys spending time with friends and clients and on making common sense more common.